BITTER MEDICINE

A Doctor's Year in Vietnam

Eugene H. Eisman, MD

The following story is true.
The names have not been changed to protect the innocent.
There are no innocents.

TABLE OF CONTENTS

Acknowledgements 5

Friendly Fire 6

Author's Note 7

PART ONE   The Unlikely Soldier   10
  Chapter 1   Doomed   11

PART TWO   Pleiku   20
  Chapter 2   Outside the Real World   21
  Chapter 3   This is Not Summer Camp   32
  Chapter 4   I Have to Vent   46
  Chapter 5   The Middle of Nowhere   51
  Chapter 6   Still No Urine   57

PART THREE   Cam Ranh   72
  Chapter 7   China Beach   73
  Chapter 8   Hawaii R & R   89
  Chapter 9   Meet Nurse Nark   97
  Chapter 10   The Hookers of Boun Me Thuot   103
  Chapter 11   Major Eisman & the Junkie Revolt 113
  Chapter 12   Home for the Moment   121
  Chapter 13   Back to Hell   125
  Chapter 14   I'm Not Dead   130

Epilogue   132

DEDICATION

This book is dedicated to the medical people who served in Vietnam. To the doctors who did not run to Canada and to the nurses who witnessed horror that will haunt them the rest of their lives. It is also dedicated to the nurses, doctors, and corpsmen who lost their lives ministering to the injured.

ACKNOWLEDGEMENTS

I am heavily indebted to those who assisted me with this manuscript, and encouraged me to write this book. Over the years I have relayed these stories to my friends who would respond, "Boy! You should write a book." I would respond that thousands of guys had the same experience and it was no big deal until my friends finally convinced me that my experiences were unique, and worth sharing with my readers.

I'm especially indebted to my wife, Diane Batshaw Eisman; my daughter, Elyktra; my friend, journalist Nina L. Diamond who encouraged me to dredge up these old memories and put them to paper before my senility took hold, and who also translated my Brooklynese into English; and Janis Nark, my comrade in arms, who helped me to recall some distant memories. I am indebted to my daughter Elyktra, and a dear friend Clara Wilkerson who corrected my bumbling formatting and expressions, in my first attempt at this publication.

I have to thank my many friends, and family who encouraged me, and last, but not least, the Microsoft Spelling Checker. However, I must admit, that without Nina, my spelling checker would have lead me astray, and I would've written "heal" for "heel", and "too" for "to".

FRIENDLY FIRE

The darkness was complete. I was almost invisible, dressed in my black turtleneck and black slacks. But not invisible to the man with the infrared sniper scope and the .223 caliber M-16. The M-16 is a terrible weapon, and few survive a round to the body. I heard shots. It's not like in the movies, you don't hear bullets whizzing by. The shots in the distance could be aimed at some movement hundreds of yards from my position, or they could be aimed at me.

I was in no man's land, beyond the barbed wire perimeter of a US Army base in Vietnam. This was flat grassland, without a hint of cover. I was dressed like the enemy. At any moment the man with the sniper scope would find me, and if he didn't find me, my foot would find a mine.

This was my second night in Vietnam. Doctors are non-combatants. We are not supposed to die in a war zone, and especially when we haven't even had our first day on the job.

AUTHOR'S NOTE

More than one third of a century has passed since men fought and died in the jungles of Southeast Asia. In the end, we were beaten. In the end, it was judged an evil mistake − "The dirty little war." A big bully of a major power was trying to bend the will of a poor backward country. Instead of marching in parades, veterans returned home to be spat upon, and politicians who never wore a military uniform were elected.

In September 2001, I was a delegate for the Florida Medical Association. At our annual meeting, those who had served the military as doctors were asked to stand up and be recognized. As I stood, I felt pride in having served my country. This, in spite of it having been the "wrong war."

It has been forty years since my Vietnam experience. Now, suddenly, I have an urge to record my experiences. I am getting ancient. If I don't record those memories now, they will certainly fade with time.

In these pages you will note how few names are mentioned. This is not just to protect the innocent, as I believe that the statute of limitations must have run its course on our various military infractions. Although, without orders fabricated by "Radar," I would have a lot less to write about, so it's certainly best that our company's "Radar" remain anonymous. Few names are mentioned simply because I've forgotten almost everybody's name. It really doesn't take forty years for me to forget a name. My brain is wired so that I'm just really bad at learning names in the first place.

It was traumatic to be separated from my family, and to see the things I saw, so perhaps I wanted to forget. But I've also grown to realize that this was an enriching experience in spite of its painful memories. I constantly remind myself that when measured against the horrors of the ordinary grunt in the field, my experience was a walk in the park.

I would never volunteer for such a traumatic experience, yet I can't say, "I wish I'd never gone to Vietnam." I believe this experience had a major, positive effect on molding me into who I am today. To say I wished I never went to Vietnam would be to say that I wished I did not exist. I once read the words of a Special Forces soldier who said, "I wouldn't go back to Vietnam for a million dollars. On the other hand, I wouldn't have given up the experience for a million dollars." That's my sentiment exactly.

Why do we like to tell our war stories? How is it that when a couple of guys get together, and then discover that each has served in Korea, or Vietnam, or some other theater of war, all they can talk about is their war experiences? We bore our friends to tears. Our friends try to restrain themselves from saying, "Stop living in the past. Get a life, will you?"

I'm sure that there is hardly a person who has not seen *Saving Private Ryan.* Remember the captain? The big question his troops kept asking was, "What did you do as a civilian?" He would answer the question with silence. Near the end of the show we finally learned the answer. He had been a schoolteacher. He probably had a class of 30 or 40 kids to control and to teach. Now he was responsible for the lives of about 150 men who served under him. He was responsible for completing his mission, and he was responsible for doing this with as few deaths as possible. Instead of a few books under his arm, he carried a .45 at his side. He was given the license not only to use his personal weapon, but also to wield the power of 150 men with their devastating mortars and automatic weapons. If he had survived, what would happen to him after his service? Why, he would return to being a schoolteacher. Just as the guy flying the B52 might return to work in the hardware store.

There is no daily experience as intense as being in a war zone. I can say this, even after serving a year in which I saw no combat and I had little risk to my personal safety.

War is horrible. Young men and woman are killed. Many survive with their lives, but are left without limbs or intact minds. Psychotherapists who specialize in Post-traumatic Stress Disorder (PTSD) serve in VA hospitals all over the United States. The wives and husbands left behind are not intact either. So how can I tell funny stories? Because amidst all the horror, the strange and unexpected and absurd also happens, war has been the fodder for the Ernie Pyles, and for *M*A*S*H*. Just a little bit of exaggeration and you have *Mr. Roberts*, and *McHale's Navy*. "Stuff" happened on an almost daily basis, and many times I caught myself thinking, "Where am I? Are they running film? Is this real life? Am I in a movie or on TV?"

Unfortunately, I wasn't.

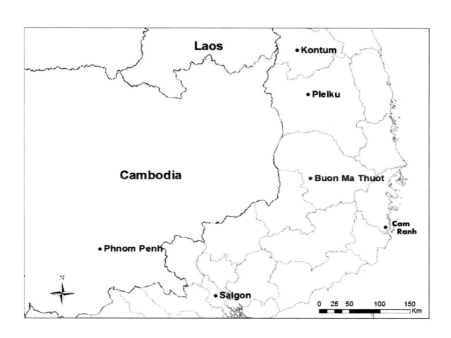

I - THE UNLIKELY SOLDIER

CHAPTER 1

DOOMED

I was at the University of Kentucky College of Medicine in the 1960s, and anxious to complete my training and become a cardiologist in private practice. Kentucky was not my real home. I was born in New York City, but had lived in Miami Florida since 1945. Not exactly a country boy. I was a bit older than most of my classmates since I had stopped along the way to get an MS in Organic Chemistry. That took an extra 3 years, and with all my debts, I owed my soul to the company store.

Even so, I was still younger than "the old man" in the class. The "old man" had blond hair and chiseled features, and had been a navy pilot before going to medical school. Instead of trying to land on the deck of a carrier that was pitching and rolling in rough seas, he was flying a desk in a classroom. We called him Steve Canyon. I don't think I'd ever known his real name while we were in med school together. Years later, looking at a class photo, I still could not remember his name. I wanted to move back to Miami and practice medicine before I, too, became the "old man." Besides, medical school is expensive, and I had debt that was piling up interest. I needed to start earning money, and begin paying back some very hungry bankers. The last thing I needed was another delay. I didn't plan to join the Army. You don't pay back about $80,000 with an army salary (about $200,000 by the year 2000).

The Army didn't care about my debt, or the bankers. That could wait. The army needed doctors, and we med students were given a choice. Did we want to be drafted after our internships and become General Medical Officers, or did we want to continue through our residency specialty training and then put in some time with Uncle Sam? A General Medical Officer would most likely be right where the fighting is. He'd be trying to patch up GIs in a tent full of bullet holes. It was either that or examining five hundred healthy men each day to determine if they were suitable for active duty. Die from a bullet wound or die of boredom — my choice.

Our other option, continuing through residency, meant signing up for the Berry Plan: Agreeing to accept a commission as an officer in the Army upon finishing residency training. You were committed for two years, but as a specialist, you would most likely be stationed in a hospital rather than a foxhole. All of us would rather work as specialists in the Army rather than be GMOs. I signed the documents and I was allowed to complete my two years of internal medicine residency, and my one-year of cardiology fellowship. Now I belonged to Uncle Sam.

Upon reading my orders, I was surprised to see that I was classified as an OBV-2. These cryptic initials stand for "obligate volunteer." Only the government could invent such a term. They knew that I volunteered, but only until they almost twisted my arm clean off. The other terms in my orders were not a surprise. My first station was to be Vietnam. The rest of my orders were unintelligible. The army loves abbreviations, and 90% of the words in my orders were cryptic abbreviations. I guess if you're regular army, and read these documents every day, they make sense. I couldn't make any sense of any of it. The word "Vietnam" was nowhere in the document. "RVN" was printed all over the paper, and I recognized that as the abbreviation for "Republic of Vietnam." The rest of the document was gobbledygook. I knew I was doomed.

Of course, first I had to pass a physical exam. As I was standing around in my underwear, I struck up a conversation with the guy next to me. I found out that he had Hemophilia, a hereditary disease in which you bleed into all your tissues after the slightest trauma. We had a long discussion, and finally placed a side bet that he would end up in Airborne. When they examined me, it was discovered that I had difficulty tracking with both eyes. "We'd better look this up to see if you're qualified to serve," said the general medical officer. He opened this big book, and read the rule to me. "As a physician, you must be blind in one eye, and losing the sight in the second eye in order to be disqualified from service." They didn't care at all about flat feet. Again, I was doomed.

It was June 1969. My wife, Diane had just finished her internship in medicine, and we had hoped to open a practice together. My daughter was only 5 years old, and she didn't want to lose her daddy. I didn't want to go, and my family didn't want me to go. The separation was painful. My brother-in-law, an attorney, said he knew how I could get out of serving. I didn't want to go, but I also had limits on what stunts I was willing to pull to stay out.

I knew it was a fruitless mission, but at my father's urging I flew to Washington to plead my case. It was not that I wanted to renege on my contract, but why did I have to go to Vietnam? Didn't they need cardiologists closer to home? Maybe they could use me at the air base in Homestead, Florida. At that time I didn't know the difference between an air base and an army base. Surely, in Vietnam they needed cardiovascular surgeons, not internists and cardiologists. I didn't have the foggiest notion how to manage anybody who was shot in the heart. My father was ill with ischemic heart disease, and he'd had a couple of small strokes while I was in medical training. Surely, they wouldn't separate me from my family.

I'd never been to Washington before. The government buildings that lined the midway were awe-inspiring. I was able to run into a few of the buildings at the Smithsonian to see some of the exhibits before my appointment. Finally, my time ran out. I found the building, and at the appointed time I presented myself to some guy in uniform sitting behind a desk. He interviewed me, and I relayed my hard luck story. Then he stood up, and said only one sentence, "If you're ordered to go, you will go, won't you?"

He was wearing a spotless white dress uniform. I was not familiar with military accoutrements, but I could see from his ribbons that he'd been everywhere, and had risked his life in every theater of war imaginable. I didn't want to go. I was scared, but there was only one response I could give, and not feel like a total piece of shit. "Of course I'll go."

From doctor to soldier…

How do you convert a bunch of doctors into a group of military officers in just a few weeks? The answer: it really can't be done. Not only is the time too short, but also doctors are extremely independent and can't take orders no matter how they try.

We were sent to Fort Sam Houston in San Antonio, Texas for our training. My wife and daughter accompanied me, and we found a little apartment. After all, pretty soon I would be gone for a long time.

They actually tried to get us to march in a straight line, and turn in the right direction upon command. They were able to teach us how to pin the various insignia on our uniforms, to salute, and to be able to tell our left foot from our right foot at least 50% of the time. When we were marching, the other officers would watch us with this expression of disbelief on their faces. We were the most unmilitary group of officers they'd ever seen. Doctors tend to be individuals even in a group. We can't march, and we can't stand at attention. It's in our genes. We went to class to learn a little bit about command skills. This was really pointless. Despite our lofty Army titles as doctors, we were joining the Army as Captains. We would be entirely out of the chain of command. If there ever were a disaster, and the general, colonels, captains and lieutenants were all killed, the private first class would be in command, and I would follow his lead. You may find extensive fault with the Army, but in this decision, regarding command, I could see nothing but great wisdom.

After our stint on the parade ground, and classroom, they sent us for weapons training to a place called Camp Bullis. It was aptly named. This place was in the middle of the unbelievably hot Texas desert, with nothing but rocks, sand, and some tumbleweed. I suppose that if a bullet went astray, it would have nothing to hit within a hundred miles except for a cactus. It is here where we learned what an M--16 can do.

The small mass of the bullet counted for little. The high velocity was everything. Now I understood what the velocity squared in $E = \frac{1}{2} Mv^2$ really meant. This equation, a generalized expression for Einstein's $E = Mc^2$ showed how important velocity was. Adding mass to a bullet would increase its energy of impact, but by adding velocity, instead of mass, you added energy to the second order of magnitude.

Our instructors anesthetized goats, and then shot them with an M--16. The bullet, traveling 3600 feet per second, drilled a small hole only ¼ inch in diameter through the animal. We dissected away the skin and could see that the tissue looked perfectly normal except for the hole. But when we'd touch the flesh, everything would fall apart. We then realized that for several inches around the small hole, the muscle had been turned to mush. The energy of the round was so great that it fractured bone and pulverized muscle in the area quite a distance from its path.

We were shown this horror not to mistreat poor defenseless animals, but to impress upon us that we should never be cavalier when evaluating a wounded soldier. Any bullet wound, no matter how small, would cause a great deal of damage, and require extensive debridement. If you didn't learn this lesson, you were likely to leave dead tissue behind, guaranteeing the perfect breeding ground for infection.

When they fired an M-16 at a big tree, the bullet went right through. The lesson? Don't bother to hide behind trees. The round will go right through a Sequoia. They fired at a can of sauerkraut with a .22 rifle, and drilled a hole through it. Then they used an M --16, and the can exploded. Even though the round of an M--16 is only about as big as a .22, this was another demonstration of the M --16's enormous energy.

We were told that the art of war was to maim and not to kill. If you killed one man that's one man out of the fight, but if you caused serious injury, you took three guys out of the fight. Then the enemy had to use up all sorts of medical facilities in an attempt to keep him alive. That is the art of war, and that was what both sides were up against.

They taught us how to behave toward friendly Vietnamese, so that we wouldn't make any horrible social blunders. These included little things, such as motioning to a waiter by waving with your fingers facing toward the floor. If we took the Western approach and waved with our fingers to the ceiling, we'd be considered insulting. In Vietnamese culture, it means you're waving to an animal. Placing your chopsticks in the rice so that the chopsticks stood straight up, meant "death," and was an insult to the host. The "ugly American" was a well-known concept at this time, and we didn't need to reinforce it, and there was no language training. In spite of this, I quickly learned the pigeon French for "pain", "bad", and other important medical terms.

We were also taught that many Vietnamese who acted like our friends might not turn out to be that friendly after all. We were entertained with diagrams showing the enemy's many ingenious booby traps.

We were told to watch our gas caps. Cleverly, the enemy was known to tie down the lever of a grenade with a rubber band, pull the pin, and then drop it into your gas tank. The gasoline would slowly dissolve the rubber, thus releasing the lever. Kaboom! How long can you watch your gas cap?

It's amazing what you can do with a trip wire. They covered every conceivable trip wire device, so that we were afraid to step off the plane.

We also learned how to handle an M-14 and a Colt .45 without shooting a toe off. The M-14 is a big, heavy rifle from the Korean War. To my knowledge, it wasn't issued to anybody in Vietnam. In training we never got to fire an M --16, I guess every last one was being used in Vietnam. I hope they never issued those Colt .45s to our fighting men. They rarely got through a magazine without jamming. Furthermore, the parts fitted so loosely that the weapon would rattle when you shook it. This made it extremely inaccurate, so that I couldn't hit a man-sized target at twenty feet. As inexperienced as I am with firearms, I know that I'm a much better shot than that.

They even had us crawl under automatic fire to give us a sense of combat. Of course, the machine gun was fixed so that it fired at least eighteen inches above the ground. That way if anybody was stupid enough to lift their head up a couple of inches, a bullet wouldn't take it clean off. I guess they felt that doctors were in short supply, and were doing their best not to kill us. Explosive charges were triggered as we crawled past just for added effect, so we were warned not to crawl over the areas that had been marked, since these were the places where the explosives had been buried. This instruction was repeated several times: "Do not crawl over the areas that we marked off. If you do this, and we hit the switch, we will blow you to little pieces." A very effective warning.

They told us that this training would protect us and help us protect our patients. If our hospital was over-run, we were expected to grab a weapon and fight to the end. I don't think anybody took this seriously.

A few of the docs refused to take any of the weapons training. They said they were willing to go to Vietnam, and serve their country by taking care of the wounded, but they wouldn't pick up a weapon and take a life under any circumstance. I can't understand their philosophy. If I, or a member of my family, were threatened, I would fight like hell. I'm ashamed to say that some physicians refused to go at all. They ran off to the hills to hide. Canada was very popular.

To protect our hearing on the firing range, we were given wax earplugs. I managed to get the plug so far in that I couldn't extract it from my ear. They had to transport me back to the infirmary where a GMO (general medical officer) removed it with forceps. Talk about really feeling stupid. One of my cohorts on this trip had an even less pleasant experience: He climbed into his sleeping bag and was stung by a scorpion.

We were also trained to read a map. Did they expect us, as Captains, to lead a company of men through the jungle? To test us, they drove us out to the desert on a dark night. We were dropped off in groups of five and given a compass, a map, and a flashlight, and a stern warning not to turn on the flashlight except to signal for help.

In the drizzle, and with no moon, it didn't take us long to figure out how worthless a compass and a map are without any light. So we disobeyed those idiotic orders, and we used our flashlights. After hours of falling into ravines, and stumbling over armadillos, we finally found our way back to the base. A few of the groups followed their orders to the letter. They didn't turn on their lights, and of course, unable to read map or compass, they couldn't find their way back. The Army had to send helicopters to look for them.

The days flew by at an unbelievable speed. Diane and I realized that our separation was imminent, and all sorts of wild plans flew through our minds. I had a cousin who had just left for Vietnam. To be with her husband, also a physician, she got a position with a church missionary service, and followed him to Vietnam. Later, I found out that they were never stationed in the same town. On rare occasions, in order to have some time together, they had to wrangle transportation through some pretty dangerous territory.

They needed doctors in Vietnam, right? What about getting two for the price of one? Diane would volunteer to go with me, just like my cousin had done with her husband. Well, that was not so simple. If she went as a civilian, she would be paying for her transportation and her own support while she was overseas. It wasn't so easy to get a job like my cousin had. Not only were we not wealthy, we were many thousands of dollars in debt. There was another factor, one that I never voiced: A civilian volunteer does not have military support. Vietnam was dangerous for anyone. Imagine an American civilian woman living there by herself. The danger would be increased by a factor of ten, at least. Then there were the living conditions. You don't exactly live a life of comfort in the Army, but life for a civilian, in the bush, would've been really primitive.

Hey! She could enlist! We would go in on the buddy system. Then we talked with people in the know. They were unanimous. No matter what the Army agreed upon, and no matter what they signed, Diane and I were sure to become separated. We were told over and over again: "Do not trust any promises from the Army." We heard all sorts of stories about married couples in the service. The husband would be stationed in the States, and the wife would be sent to Vietnam. A year would pass and then the wife would come home and it was the husband's turn to go to Vietnam. We also had a five-year-old daughter. We would have to leave her with her grandparents for at least a year. This was a stressful time, and our thinking was mostly selfish, but in the back of our minds we realized that both of my daughter's parents would be at risk, and it would not be inconceivable that she could be orphaned because of our decision.

Leaving on a Jet Plane…

When it was time to leave our stateside training base, I had some mixed feelings. I knew that I had to go, and I would be gone for one year. The sooner I left, the sooner I could return. Nobody likes the pain of saying good-byes. There is so much you want to say, but you know that you have to keep your mouth shut. You have to think of your partner's pain also. You don't want to be killed, but their fear of being left alone — perhaps having to bring up a family by their lonesome is much worse. At the airport, I was actually anxious to get through the goodbyes, get on the plane, and get the clock ticking.

I was surprised to find that we newly minted "soldiers" flew by commercial carrier (I was hoping to get to fly in a B-52). It turned out to be Continental Airlines. The planes were a bit of a surprise, however. Maybe I was hallucinating, but it appeared to me that they cut the plane in half. Then they put another fuselage between the two halves, and welded it to create a plane that was twice as long. It looked funny, like a stretch limousine with short, little wings. I was quite surprised when it actually managed to take off.

I sat in the approximate center of the aircraft. In each direction I saw rows of guys in class A uniforms.

We had three classes of uniforms: There was the dress uniform, which I never bought. I knew I would never be called on to wear fancy dress stuff. There was combat fatigues – the name says everything, and there was class A, which is the uniform to be worn in civilian areas. I got to wear that uniform in my second year of service. I was stationed in Fort Jackson, South Carolina.

The plane was filled with young warriors. All their expressions were the same: somber. Nobody spoke, and except for the engines, everyone was silent. It was a long flight from the known, familiar world to the great unknown.

I left on September 11, 1970. That meant I was scheduled to return on September 10, 1971, my DEROS. DEROS is another strange military acronym. I believe it means "Date of Estimated Return Overseas," but I wouldn't swear by it. I've checked both the *Oxford Dictionary* and the *Webster Unabridged Dictionary*, and there is nothing between "Deroge" and "Derotremate."

II - PLEIKU

CHAPTER 2

OUTSIDE THE REAL WORLD

DAY ONE – Another World

I think we landed in Bien Hoa. This is pronounced **Ben Wa**. For the next twelve months, I would have to learn how to pronounce strange words that seemed to have little relationship to their spelling. All I could remember was that it was a 14-hour flight, but I guess that our destination is one of those things that have faded from my memory. I remember sitting in a small room at the 90th Replacement. We had all flown in wearing class "A" uniforms. These uniforms are not suitable for a combat area, so the first thing they did was issue us the clothing that we would be wearing for the year we were in Vietnam. We were issued fatigues, the Army's equivalent of Levis, two pairs of jungle boots, and our underwear. Even though most of Vietnam is tropical, the Army issue shirts were all long sleeved heavy cotton to give us some protection from the mosquitos and Malaria. Everything was the same color. Even the underwear and handkerchiefs were olive drab. Later, when I went to Sabbath services, I was issued an olive drab *Tallis* (prayer shawl), in an olive drab case. They also had olive drab *yarmulkes* (skullcaps). The next time I would put on my class 'A' uniform, I was leaving Vietnam. I learned later that the women were issued olive drab bras and panties. I guess everything had to be camouflaged.

We were issued a bottle of C-P pills, tablets that were a combination of Chloroquine and Primaquine. We were to take one tablet each week to protect us from Malaria. Each week, one hour after taking our tablet, we would get ferocious cramps and diarrhea. This was only partially protective against Malaria, as some strains were extremely resistant. For that reason the grunts in the field were not issued C-P. They had to take a daily tablet of Dapsone. This is not a benign medication. Dapsone doesn't cause diarrhea. In addition to causing vomiting, it destroys your red blood cells. This hemolysis occurs in almost everybody who takes even as much as 200 mg of this drug. A few may die from this drug, but the upside is that it protects you from leprosy.

The next thing they did was to take all our money from us. They warned us that if they caught us with a single greenback, they would send us to Leavenworth. In return, they gave us this Monopoly money. I didn't figure out how all this worked until much later. This system was to prevent real money from falling into the hands of the enemy. You can't buy real guns and real bullets with Monopoly money

Somehow, the North Vietnamese still managed to do this without our real dollars.

Every few weeks they would announce that our money, whatever color it was, would be worthless the next day. We would have to line up with our blue Monopoly money, and the cashier would exchange it for red Monopoly money. The idea was that if you were paid $1000 per month, and had $20,000 in your possession, you had some explaining to do. This way, if you made a killing on the black market, you would have a choice between being left with a lot of worthless Army Monopoly money, or ten years in Leavenworth. Of course you could send your money home, but where could your girlfriend spend the Army's Monopoly money?

While I was in Vietnam, they pulled this Monopoly money color switch on us about four times. This essentially caught the Black Marketers with their pants down. However, I compared notes with a friend who spent 1967 in Korea. There they pulled the switch on currency only once. In Korea, the whole thing was a laugh, and according to him, American currency flowed freely.

After we packed our duffels, we were sent into a room where a regular army officer type stood at a podium and the ten of us officers sat "in the audience." Our names were called out, and we were all given our assignments. We were each assigned to a different station. I was told to "be in Pleiku tomorrow."

A member of the audience made the serious error of asking, "How do we get to our stations?"

The answer was simple. "You're big boys, find your own way."

Vietnam was a war torn country, and without front lines. There were no "safe" areas. Each of us, traveling alone, was expected to find a helicopter, a fixed wing, or a convoy and hitch a ride. No wonder the guys in M*A*S*H* stole a jeep to get to the base. Missing jeeps were such a serious problem in Vietnam that signs were posted all over the place: "IF YOU STEAL A JEEP, YOU GO TO JAIL."

That night we were sent off to a group of giant tents, to bed down on cots with old, torn sheets for cover until morning, when we would travel to our posts. The tents were in a swamp. Boards had been thrown over the mud so we could get to the tents. How nice of them. The mosquitoes were ferocious, and seemed to be the size of B17s. I was up for hours trying to swat them away. More than once I thought, "If I get malaria, I'm fucked."

Finally, I walked off into the darkness to find the supply room. This was tricky. It would have been easy to miss a step, walk off the board into the mud, and sink out of sight. After wandering across a maze of planks, I found a hut with a half door, and a board for a counter over the half door. I explained to the sergeant behind the counter, "The mosquitos are murder, can you give me a can of repellant?"

He handed me a khaki aerosol container in the semi darkness, and I wandered back into the blackness to find my tent. I sprayed myself from head to toe with this foul smelling stuff. I sprayed twice, even though it smelled like gasoline – just to make certain that I hadn't missed a spot. It worked! No mosquitos bothered me that night. I just prayed that nobody would light a match. In the light of the morning, I was able to read the label: "INSECTICIDE."

Once again, I thought: "I'm doomed." I'll probably die from the neurotoxin in about three days.

DAY TWO Lost in Pleiku

The first few days are the biggest culture shock that anybody could expect to tolerate. In Vietnam, the official word for home was CONUS, or Continental United States. The common term for home however was "The Real World." This was for good reason. Vietnam was as strange to us as the planet Mars. People have asked me if I was frightened. We were all too stunned to be frightened. It was like walking through a dream. You felt like you'd lost all control of your life, which was perfectly true. The Army told you what to do, and when to do it. Sometimes this was a good thing. If you didn't feel that somebody was in control, you might totally decompensate in such a strange situation. This was total unreality.

The next morning, looking for a way to get to my base, I found a C-130 (I think). The multiengine plane had a big trap door in the back to load cargo, or to allow the airborne to parachute out of this perfectly good plane. Before boarding, seven of us were lined up outside next to the trap door and we were all asked our weight. What would happen if I lied? If I told them that I weighed 175 and I really weighed 185, would we fall out of the sky because they didn't load enough fuel?

Then the pilot gave us a briefing: "If you hear a single blast on the horn, it means we're having trouble on the runway. Evacuate the plane immediately. If you hear two blasts on the horn, it means we're airborne and we are having problems. We have three parachutes. The flight crew will use the parachutes to get help."

They looked too serious to be kidding.

For the rest of my tour in Vietnam, the most common "bus" I used for getting from one part of the country to the other was the C130. The HU1 helicopter was great for transporting the wounded from the battlefield, but when I needed to accompany a patient to the Saigon Field Hospital, the C130 was our transportation. The Army used it to move troops, sometimes landing them on some distant airfield, but sometimes just dropping that big rear door and having them use their parachutes. The C130 was also converted to a gun-ship. Designated the AC130H Spectre, it was the terror of the North Vietnamese soldier. A jet fighter would make a single run on the ground troops, and then after quickly exhausting its fuel and ammunition, return to base. The AC130H was a turboprop, so it could stay over the battlefield for hours. In what was called a Pylon turn, it would circle the area, banked so that the cannons mounted on the fuselage could direct their fire to the same area, and absolutely sterilize it. It carried many thousands of rounds of 20mm ammunition, and a later version of this plane even carried a 105mm Howitzer. Darkness didn't matter. The AC130 carried the most advanced radar and night vision sighting equipment. The grunts had a pet name for this bird. They called him, "Puff the Mighty Dragon."

The C130 was not the most comfortable way to fly. This was not a commercial 747, with plush seats, bathrooms fore and aft, and pretty stewardi. You sunk your rear end into plastic webbing that was designed to encompass a parachute. The trouble was, we were not wearing parachutes, so here we sat with our butts practically touching the deck, and our knees almost touching our chins. I never appreciated the noise insulation found on commercial jets until I flew that C130. The engine noise was deafening, and even screaming into your partner's ear, it was impossible to carry on a conversation. It was a good thing we had nothing to say to each other. We were all lost in our own thoughts, and I'm sure that everyone thought the same thing: "What the hell am I doing here?" Thankfully, the flight was short. I was actually able to stand up again when we reached Pleiku.

I had pictured Pleiku as a little military town. I was surprised that it appeared to be the size of Miami, Florida. The runway was not made of concrete; it was made of steel plate. This was needed to support the giant C5A. These cargo planes were monsters — you could park a 747 under each wing.

Outside the terminal, I saw a couple of military types climbing into a jeep.

"Where is the dispensary?" I asked. "I'm the new doc."

"Great!" One of them exclaimed. "We need another doc. Come with us."

And off I went in their jeep. Pleiku was big, and their base was not very close. I didn't know where we were going, but about this time I had lost all hope of ever having control over my fate again. I just sat back and thought, "I don't know who these guys are. Maybe I'll end up as a doctor for the Vietcong."

I sat back in the jeep, and tried to soak up all the scenery. I passed hundreds of army trucks, row after row of tanks, and mountains of supplies. It looked like the whole war effort was supplied from this busy place. I remember seeing a few Vietnamese workers, but otherwise, this city was a giant American supply base – a major American city right in the middle of another country.

After about an hour of driving through this city of armament, we reached the headquarters, and I was advised to introduce myself to the colonel.

"Who is this?" he asked.

"He's our new doc," one of my new friends explained.

I stood there watching them talk about me. I felt like a little child tagging after some adults who were in control. I was certainly not in control, and I felt I should be holding a lollypop.

"What the hell are you talking about?" the colonel barked. "He's wearing the wrong uniform."

Then I thought, "Well, they can't be the Vietcong. Those are certainly American uniforms, and they sure speak perfect English."

"Can't you see he's Army? We are Air Force, you numbskulls."

"Can't we keep him?" they pleaded.

Images of a stray puppy flashed across my brain.

"No, you can't keep him, the colonel said. "Take him back where he belongs."

Late in the afternoon, I finally reached the 71st Evac, my home for the next 6 months. It was located on a plateau in the central highlands, an area designated as I Corp by the US Armed Forces. We called it "Eye Corp." There were four Corps in Vietnam. Using unbelievable imagination, they were called Corp I, Corp II, Corp III, and Corp IV.

I was introduced to the two other docs, and then was told that I was on call for the emergency room my first night.

My new buddies invited me out to the bar. "But, I'm on call!" I exclaimed.

"It's always quiet in the ER, and we're not going very far. Come with us to the Air force club. The Army's joint is a hole-in-the-wall."

My second day in Vietnam, and I was already introduced to the differences between the Army, Navy, and Air Force. Oh, I know they do different things. The Air Force flies planes (although the army has invaded this territory now), and the Navy sails boats. But the way they treat their men was different, too. The Army supplies the most primitive quarters, and the bare-bones luxury that can hardly be called officer's clubs. I had the opportunity to visit the navy and airforce bases. Their officer's clubs had excellent cuisine. The buildings were permanent structures of concrete and steel. Both, at Pleiku and at Cam Ranh, the building were mostly wood or Quonset huts. Neither the Sixth Convalescent Center or the 71 st Evac had anything you could call an Officer's Club.

So, I followed my new friends down a road, past the barbed wire and past the guards. We were walking over perfectly flat grassland on this gigantic plateau. Off in the distance were guard towers, and further away were the mountains that surrounded us. The mountains appeared small in the distance. We were on top of one of the highest ones, and there were not many to be seen that were higher than ours. After a couple of miles we could see a one story, unpainted, weathered building sitting out on the plain. We had finally reached the Officers Club of the Air Force. The so-called club was just a dingy bar with a few tables, and a small dance floor. That meant the Army club back at the dispensary must have been even worse. I sat at the bar and had a beer with my buddies. It soon became obvious that alcohol was the main entertainment outlet for GIs. An hour later, the bartender picked up the phone. "It's a call for the doc. They have somebody at the ER."

My friends offered to walk me back, but I wasn't one to ruin their evening. "Look, I can find my way back," I said. "I'll just follow the road."

My friends were insistent. "Are you sure?" they kept asking.

I couldn't understand why they were so insistent on escorting me. What was the big deal? The dispensary was only a couple of miles down the road. I insisted on going alone.

I step outside, and it's dark. Not the kind of darkness you see at night back home in CONUS. But dark dark. Like the darkness you see in a photographic dark room. There are no lights on in Vietnam at night (You wanna get killed?). Not only is it dark, it's raining. And there's no moon or even a star in the sky. It's beyond dark.

I start to walk. I can't see my hand in front of my face, but I can feel the road under my feet. Pretty soon I feel a change in the terrain. I am no longer walking on asphalt, but on grass. I've wandered off the road. Now I don't have the foggiest idea where the road is, and I can't retrace my steps. Periodically, I hear shots. Occasionally I see tracer fire, and a flare set off in the distance. Oh crap, I'm wandering aimlessly in a free fire zone.

You do not belong in a free fire zone unless you're the enemy. Guards at the perimeter are instructed to shoot at anything they see in the free fire zone, since anything they see is unlikely to be friendly. To make matters even worse, I wasn't wearing my uniform that night. I was wearing a black turtleneck shirt and black jeans. This is the uniform of the Vietcong, the enemy. So much for dressing casually in a combat zone.

Today, thinking back to that dreadful night, I realize that I should've been terrified. Any sane person would be. I'd been traveling for days, from one strange and disorienting place to the next. When people talk about numb, this was numb. I remember calmly thinking, "What are my choices? If I continue to walk in this area, I'm likely to get shot and killed. I could sit on the ground, in the light rain, and wait for daylight, but as soon as day begins to break, they'll spot me and certainly shoot me." I remember feeling no fear. But not out of bravery, out of psychosis. By now I'd lost all of my reality testing abilities. General Eisenhower was well aware of this state of mind when he planned the invasion of Normandy. He was careful to choose only green troops, troops that had never seen action, for his landing force. He knew that battle hardened men would recognize the type of odds they were facing, and many would freeze and would never leave the landing craft.

Finally, I found the road. What a relief! Then I walked into accordion wire— barbed wire that's been pulled off the roll so that it lies in giant spirals. The road was completely blocked by this razor sharp wire. Wrong road!

I turned around and again wandered aimlessly. I expected to get shot at any moment. Again I began debating with myself whether I should just lie down on the wet ground and wait for morning. Maybe if I played dead nobody would shoot me. Then I found another road. It took a few hours, but I finally reached the ER. I caught hell for taking so long to respond to the call, but I was happy that I hadn't caught a round from an M--16.

So ended the first night at my new home, at my new job.

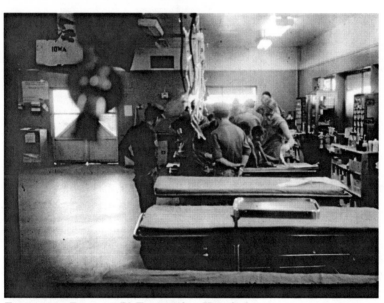

Emergency Room at 71 Evacuation Hospital.

C-128 served as much of my transportation.

Montagnards visiting family at the 71st Evac.

Chinook utilized when there were many casualties.

CHAPTER 3

THIS IS NOT SUMMER CAMP

The set-up of the North Vietnamese Army is a bit confusing. It's fragmented, to say the least. The "regular" North Vietnamese Army was called the PAVN, or the Peoples' Army of Vietnam. The Viet Cong, also called the National Liberation Front, or NLF, was a bit more of a mystery. It was considered by some as a "branch" of the PAVN whose duties were strictly guerrilla. Many insisted that the Viet Cong was an insurgency strictly indigenous to the south. However, the general feeling was that both the PAVN and the VC, were under the same command structure.

My home, in this strange world, was called a "hootch." It was a hut divided into six rooms. Each of six officers had a room measuring 6 x 8 feet. Each room had one window and a couple of shelves on the wall. There were three rooms on each side of a long hallway with a communal bathroom at the end. The hootch was a flimsy thing made of plywood and two by fours. Since the walls weren't hollow, there was no insulation. I quickly grew to appreciate the relative luxury of this life. The enlisted men were housed in a barn-like structure where about one hundred cots were arranged in neat rows. Only 3 feet separated each cot. I would've gone nuts with such a lack of privacy. This was the first time that I truly appreciated the advantage of being an officer.

Our little hospital was staffed with three surgeons, two internists (including myself), an ophthalmologist, and an anesthesiologist. The Commander was one of the surgeons, and he saw his share of operations. There must have been a supporting staff of about fifty including about twenty nurses. The hospital was the equivalent of a MASH unit, but with a major difference. It was no longer a *Mobile* Army Surgical Hospital, and the tents had long been replaced with corrugated steel walls and roofs. A building of about 150 feet by 100 feet housed an operating room, emergency room, and a ward of about forty beds. About twenty smaller buildings served as hootches for the doctors and nurses, and also a Headquarters building. We also had a Mess, and a small chapel. A chain link fence topped with accordion wire surrounded the compound.

Sandbags surrounded the walls of my hootch, but although these sandbags wouldn't protect us from a direct hit, or even a near miss, we might expect some protection from small arms fire, or shrapnel from a grenade. My hootch was near the barbed wire perimeter. Just outside that fence stood a piece of mobile artillery. I don't know the diameter of the shell it fired, but it must've been a big one. At odd hours, in the middle of the night, with an ear splitting boom, this monster would fire a round over my hootch. My breath would stop and my whole body would rise a few inches above the bed. Since I'd never know when it would come, it was always quite a loud surprise. No matter how late I slept, I always felt a bit sleep deprived. This was a military sleep apnea. On return from Vietnam I became aware of a hearing loss. I began with VA hearing aids, but now I'm as deaf as a stone. Hearing aids are completely ineffective, and now I have had surgery for cochlear implants.

My bed was just a thin mattress on a sheet of corrugated steel, supported on three sides by sandbags. One side was left open so that I could dive under the bed when attacked. This was of small comfort. I know the bed sounds a bit uncomfortable, but when compared with the army cots used by the enlisted men, it was pure luxury.

Even though we were in the central highlands, a combat hot area, we felt rather secure since our base was a hospital and we had a gigantic radar array. The theory was that the North Vietnamese army would spare us so that they could get this radar installation intact when we left. They knew that we would leave someday, and we knew that they were right.

I didn't exactly feel at home. I was born in New York City, moved to Miami, and in general spent most of my life in big cities. When I was a Cub Scout in Coney Island, we never went hiking or camping. The only place you can pitch a tent in Brooklyn is in an alley. This is not too safe. The "wildlife" in Brooklyn is far more dangerous than the wildlife in the woods. I had never camped overnight in my whole life. Now I was camping on a high plateau, and as I gazed past the barbed wire on the perimeter, I could see hundreds of miles in all directions. All I saw was the green of endless, dense jungle. This was not the right environment for a city boy.

When I was in medical school, in Kentucky, I would occasionally explore the state and national parks. At the top of Natural Bridge, in Kentucky, the scenery was much the same as in Vietnam: green everywhere. There was a difference, however. In Kentucky, it was thousands of acres of beautiful forest, teeming with wild animals who just wanted to be left alone. In Vietnam, it was thousands of acres of triple canopied jungle, teeming with people who wanted to kill you.

I had some previous exposure to life and medicine in the "sticks." While I was a medical resident, I earned some pocket money by working weekends for a physician in Campton, Kentucky. I was in the only medical office in a 45-mile radius, and the nearest hospital was the University of Kentucky Medical Center 75 miles away. We would see as many as 250 patients a day since there was no other medical facility in the neighborhood. People would stream in 24 hours a day, and I actually slept in the clinic.

I had another experience in rural medicine before joining the Army. During the three-month hiatus between my completion of medical training and my call to active duty, I had found work in a little town in rural eastern Kentucky. The obstetrician at their small hospital had not had a vacation in seven years, and they begged me to come.

"But, I just finished my cardiology fellowship. I'm not an ob-gyn." I explained.

They were desperate. They assured me that I would have full hospital privileges in ob-gyn, and they would get me malpractice coverage. I was a little crazier in those days, and I actually accepted the job.

***

I ate at the officer's mess. You'd think that because you belonged to Uncle Sam, he'd pick up the tab, but not if you're an officer. I was surprised to find that I had to pay for my meals in Military Payment Certificates (MPCs). You got a free meal only if you were a non-commissioned officer or a grunt. Our officer's salary was quite adequate, especially since we had nowhere to spend our money. Most of my money was deposited stateside, so that my wife and child could survive. The rest of the money was issued to me in MPCs.

Our MPC was good at the local PX where we could buy some toiletries, and a few luxuries such as simple, inexpensive cameras. A big PX could be found in Hong Kong, or Thailand. When going on R & R, you were allowed to take real money. Everybody wanted a hi-fi set in their hootch. What else could you do in your off hours but listen to music? We also wanted to record our experiences and send pictures home. Nikon Cameras were surprisingly inexpensive since we could get them at a PX duty free and tax-free. Anybody going on R & R was loaded down with cash and lists from all his friends. It was his job to lug all the goodies back to the base.

When I arrived in Vietnam, all I carried was my duffle. When I left, I had to pack crates with a hi-fi set, including a large reel-to-reel tape recorder, and of course, I had my Nikon with its full complement of lenses.

Whenever we'd get away from the base, we'd carry our cameras. Everybody wanted to have a record of this strange place. It was as if we all felt that if we didn't have pictures to show the folks back home, nobody would ever believe what we'd experienced. I took slides, a bad choice. Now when I want to review my shots, I have to drag out the projector. More than forty years later, the color has faded from the slides. No "digital" in those days.

My contact with the Vietnamese was with my patients at the 71st Evac. However, I had the opportunity of visiting nearby towns, and saw life outside of the hospital setting. At Buon Me Thout, about one hundred miles south of Pleiku, I saw a gathering of five teenagers, and thought it would be a good photo. When I took the shot, I thought that it was just a friendly bunch of typical kids, each with an arm about his buddy's shoulder. Even when I got the film developed, I thought it was just an ordinary photo of ordinary kids. It wasn't until I got home from Vietnam, and took a good look at the shot, that I realized what a poignant photo I had. These kids were protectively gathered around one of their own whose arm had been amputated. He probably was the victim of a mine, or bullet. There were no ordinary people in this country. They had all been exposed to destruction of homes, and if they had somehow not lost a limb or their life, they knew someone who had. I sent the photo into the Nikon contest for amateur photographers. The judges recognized what the photo represented and sent me an honorable mention. (Plate x)

We had to be careful with our little sojourns into the countryside. This was "tourist season" in Vietnam — that is, nobody had to be concerned about exceeding a limit when shooting a tourist, and we were the "tourists" in this country. On one occasion, I was exploring the local countryside with three other doctors when we stopped our jeep in the middle of a field. We were approached by a Montagnard who wanted us to join him for a drink. The Montagnards, or Mountain Men, were a primitive people who were our allies. He pointed to a thatched roof house about fifty yards away. The Montagnards had no common language, lived around their campfire, and generally owned only what they could carry on their backs. To my knowledge, they were fiercely loyal to the American and South Vietnamese side.

These people have an extremely potent rice wine that they keep in an immense jar. The clan gathers around the jar and sips the alcohol using long reeds. It was tempting, but, at that time, I felt there was no way to be certain that we were among friends, so we said no thank-you. He was displeased, and I'm sure we hurt his feelings when we turned this honor down, but we were chicken – and ignorant.

We never went very far on these little trips. I was frightened enough as it was. It was frustrating to be in a country that had such an unusual and interesting culture, and yet be too frightened to explore. This was a strange war. There were no front lines here. We controlled the cities, but outside the city, especially at night, you were in no man's land. If anybody controlled the night, anywhere, it was the Vietcong. Even in the middle of Saigon, you weren't completely safe. It was rumored that at certain bars both the North and the South ate and drank in peace, but as soon as they left, they were at war again.

Each day I would make rounds at our little 40-bed hospital. You'd think that those beds would be occupied by soldiers with gunshot wounds, but most soldiers were there for treatment of various tropical diseases. In all the wars throughout history, diseases carried by mosquitoes, lice, and ticks cause most of the casualties. Half of my patients were Vietnamese. I can't speak Vietnamese, and the only thing else they could speak was a pidgin French. I learned the important things, like the word for pain. I saw disease in stages that you'd never witness in the United States. Village people knew about only one kind of doctor: the witch doctor. I remember an elderly Montagnard who had a goiter the size of a grapefruit. It was so large that it kept him from lowering his chin. The surgeon wouldn't operate on his thyroid, because the patient also had severe aortic stenosis. His Aortic valve was heavily calcified, and would not open wide enough to allow adequate blood flow so that he would survive surgery. His aortic valve would have to be replaced before we could operate on his neck, and where in Vietnam could you find a bypass machine for open-heart surgery? His aortic valve disease was probably Rheumatic Heart Disease. I saw a lot of Rheumatic Fever in young Vietnamese. This disease was disappearing in the United States, probably due to our use of Penicillin, but in Vietnam the disease was rampant, dooming many youngsters to heart disease when they became older.

The rounds took only an hour or two, and then I would see our emergency room patients. The gunshot and shrapnel wounds were surgical problems, and as an internist, that was not my department.

The surgical experience was so intense that surgeons who'd interrupted their residency to go to Vietnam were given a year's credit in training for the year spent in Vietnam.

Our primary mission was to care for soldiers injured in action or made ill from hepatitis, typhus, or malaria, but we took all comers, and I'm sure that many of the Vietnamese that we cared for were actually enemies from the North. We saw diseases that physicians in the United States don't see in a lifetime of medical practice. I even saw plague.

In war, disease is a major player in the success of battle. This is ancient history where typhus and other diseases destroyed armies. However, as late as the Second World War, the Japanese were devastated in the jungles when they were not supplied with quinine to fight Malaria as were the allies. I'm sure it's still a big factor today.

During the Second World War, the Medic would care for the injured soldier in the field. The Medic was a regular soldier who had been given a quick course in how to stop a sucking wound in the chest, or control bleeding from a torn artery. After the Medic stopped the bleeding and started an intravenous line, the wounded would then be taken by ground ambulance, a so-called "cracker box," to a field hospital. You can imagine that many didn't survive the trip.

We did it differently in Korea and then in Vietnam. We still had the medic who was often addressed lovingly as "doc" by his buddies, but while he stabilized the injured, they would trigger a smoke grenade. A helicopter would report, "I see green smoke," or "I see red smoke," and the buddies would respond, "That's us." Traditionally, the medic was unarmed and well-marked with a red cross. Not all countries recognize the Geneva Conventions. The medics in Vietnam looked like everybody else, and were armed. (Plate x)

Then the helicopter would swoop down and transport the wounded. The pilot would identify the color of the smoke just before coming in so that the enemy wouldn't have a chance to release identical grenades and draw the helicopter into unfriendly territory. These helicopters could transport six to nine patients at a time inside the fuselage where first aid could be administered. (This was a great improvement over the Korean conflict, when helicopters carried only a pair of wounded in external pods.) In Vietnam the average helicopter ride would take only 35 minutes, a feat that saved many lives. Of the wounded who reached the hospital, more than 97% survived and 40% were able to return to combat. We used these helicopters to transport casualties of war, and also the ill or injured civilians to various hospitals.

Flying an air ambulance was extremely hazardous. According to the Geneva Conventions, an air ambulance is not to be fired upon as long as it registers its flight plan with the enemy. Of course, it's impossible to meet this criterion. So the unarmed helicopters, painted with red crosses, were fair game.

When I saw my first patients, I was lost. We studied these diseases in medical school, but neither the students, nor the teachers, thought that they would ever become an important part of our practice, so I had only a cursory knowledge of them. The docs who were already there when I arrived were a great help. I also had the foresight to bring a few textbooks. Let me tell you, a heavy duffle bag gets really heavy when you add about thirty pounds of books.

We also had our share of snakebites. We have a little green snake in Florida who's both harmless and cute. They also have a green snake in Vietnam, but it's venomous. We had one poor guy who stepped out of his chopper and onto a cobra. He was dead before they could medevac him.

As I said, half my patients were Vietnamese, but half of the Vietnamese were Montagnards. They were not considered Vietnamese by the rest of the population, and in fact they were discriminated against. The city people considered these mountain people subhuman. They certainly didn't look Vietnamese. They more closely resembled our Native Americans, and although olive skinned, they had occidental rather than Asiatic features. The Montagnards always smelled like smoke since they spent their lives around the campfire. Their shelter consisted of palm frond and bamboo huts raised above the ground on long poles, and they carried everything they owned on their backs. They were our allies, and had the reputation of being thoroughly trustworthy. When you treated a Vietnamese, you never could be sure whether he was from the North or the South. You never knew whether he was friend or enemy. The Montagnards were always our friends.

Our Vietnamese allies could not understand how we could be so blind. "Can't you see how different the North Vietnamese looks compared to a Southerner?"

Not me! They could not understand that to us, all Vietnamese looked alike.

****

In spite of our extensive military training (a great big several weeks), we were still unsure of army protocol. I remember sitting at the mess with a few of the other docs, when in walked a one-star general who came over to our table. Now, to me, this is like the president of General Motors coming to my table. I stand for General Motors. I stood up, but the rest of the docs remained seated. The general looked around for about one minute in total silence and then he went ballistic. Using words that are used to refer to rather private functions, and never in mixed company, he let us know that we were expected to stand in the presence of a general officer. I really couldn't blame my buddies. We had never met a general before.

****

Next to HQ, the Army was building a bunker. The walls and ceiling consisted of, first, a layer of corrugated steel, then a layer of sandbags, and then a layer of corrugated steel. This series was repeated until they had walls and a ceiling that were more than 10 feet thick.

"Boy!" I exclaimed, "Nothing could get through that. Are you expecting a Nuke?"

"Are you kidding?" responded a veteran. "That will only protect you from a near miss. The smallest rocket would blow that to hell."

That was very comforting.

I was told to always be conscious of my surroundings. Even if you don't hear any shooting, you must remember that you are in the midst of a war. I learned of a recent incident where inattention proved fatal: A doc was riding down a road on a motorbike with a nurse sitting behind him. He drove right past a guard post, thinking that it was unoccupied. The guard fired a single round from his M--16 that penetrated both riders. The bullet severed the spinal cord of the nurse, leaving her a paraplegic, and killed the doctor.

The grunts who survived learned how to never really sleep. They always had to listen for that bolt being slid closed on an AK-47 rifle or the snap of a twig. They slept with one eye open. To really go to sleep was to take the chance of waking up dead. The combatants never got to actually sleep for the entire year they were in Vietnam. This super alert state did not get turned off, even when they got back to CONUS. This was a common expression of post-traumatic stress disorder (PTSD). After my tour in the Army, I discussed this with a psychologist who specialized in PTSD. She told me about a patient of hers who could not stop walking around his block or his room. He never seemed to sit down, and when you asked him why, he would say that he was just checking the perimeter.

We rarely felt threatened, since we were in the middle of a gigantic military facility. I remember seeing only one mortar round land in our compound. At night, I would occasionally hear the scream of a Gatling gun. These machine guns were mounted on HU-1 attack helicopters. Invented during our Civil War, the Gatling consisted of about ten rifle barrels bound together. A crank was used to rotate the bundle and fire each barrel in turn. They didn't use a hand crank in the helicopters. These rotating barrels would send a solid column of steel to the ground at the rate of 3000 rounds per minute. That translates to an unbelievable 50 bullets every second. Instead of the rat-tat-tat of a typical machine gun, their super rapid fire would sound like a siren scream. These attack helicopters would patrol our perimeter at night, and anybody trying to get through the wire would be shredded.

Everybody has had the overwhelming feeling of loneliness when they leave home to go to their first summer camp. I was a big boy, but this was a big, strange, dangerous kind of camp. My body and soul belonged to the Army, which we all called "the big green machine." I couldn't feel sorry for myself for very long. I ran into this doc at the base who was a few years older than I was. I learned that he had been through the Korean War.

"So, how come you're here? You hate your family? You like these primitive conditions? You like war?" I asked him.

He told me his story. After serving in Korea as a grunt, he decided to go to medical school. He studied hard, graduated, and got ready to go into private practice. Then he got a notification from the Department of Defense. It appears that because he was now a doctor, he had incurred a new obligation, and was again subject to the draft. I thought there was a law against double jeopardy.

He was back in the service. Now at least, he was a captain rather than a grunt. He was also given a little extra pay, because of all the time he spent in service, so he came out of it with a few extra bucks in his pocket.

I was a "newbie" in the dispensary. I remember the first time I gave a GI a shot of penicillin. I casually threw the empty vial in the garbage.

"Hey, you can't do that," yelled the Corpsman.

"Why not, it's empty?"

"I'll tell you why not. The hootch maid will fish out the vial. Then she will fill it with Wild Root Cream Oil (Only us ancients remember this hair product.). Then she will sell it on the black market as penicillin. Finally, some poor jerk will get his clap treated with a shot of Wild Root Cream Oil."

He then went on to explain that you had to crush the empty vial so that it could never be used for any nefarious purpose.

I became comfortable treating Malaria and dengue. Even though this was not the stuff I saw in my residency, it was infectious disease. Dengue is also transferred by a mosquito, but it is a virus. The pain is excruciating, as you might guess from its common name, "Break Bone Fever." There are no antimicrobial drugs that are effective against Dengue. Even though this was not the stuff I saw in my residency, it was infectious disease. With a little help from textbooks, and my colleagues, I could muddle through. I learned that it wasn't easy to make a Malaria diagnosis. The books said all you had to do was take a blood sample and throw it under the microscope. Guys would come in with high, spiking fevers, and so sick they had trouble sitting up. But when we'd look under the scope, there were no parasites to be seen. I quickly learned that these little buggers could hide in various organs, and would only come out in the blood when you weren't looking. You had to get many blood samples at odd hours, before you finally caught them. Sometimes, even that failed. We would have to stick a needle in the sternum (the breast bone), and try to find them in the bone marrow.

I had real problems with the other stuff. I would be called to the ER when we had casualties but since I wasn't a surgeon, I felt helpless trying to assist people with horrible injuries. It may surprise you, but physicians who are not surgeons have a real problem looking at torn flesh, limbs ripped off, and gaping wounds. It's even more of a problem when you feel like an idiot, totally untrained for the task in front of you.

I stepped up to the stretcher of one poor soul who had both eyes lying on his cheeks. They dangled by their optic nerves.

"Don't bother with him," called a surgeon.

"Why not?" I answered.

The surgeon came over and wordlessly lifted the patient by his hair. The back of his head was gone. I didn't need words to learn this lesson. We are shorthanded. You can't waste your time on the hopeless.

One of the lessons you learn early is the principle of triage. Casualties come in overwhelming clumps. One of the surgeon's most important duties is to divide the patients into three groups: Group One was those with minor injuries. They can be told to go sit under a tree somewhere until things quiet down, and then they can come in for a couple of sutures, or whatever minor treatment they needed. Group Two was those with serious injuries that needed immediate attention. They were sent directly in for care. Group Three was those with extremely serious injuries. They were given a shot of morphine to control the pain, and put over in the corner where they could die while we took care of those who were salvageable. To the layperson, the system seems callous, but this is what you need to do to save as many lives and limbs as possible. You're in a place that does not have unlimited medical facilities, and where the use of time and talent must be efficiently utilized. This was where you learned about the real cruelty of war, the stuff that cannot be described in the movies. This is where you see the real pain, and the utterly stupid waste of youth and life.

I am now on the staff of several civilian hospitals. In each emergency room there is a triage nurse. She is the first nurse you will see, and she will decide whether you fall into Group One and can sit in the waiting room, or in Group Two and should be seen in the ER immediately. In a modern hospital, under normal conditions, major effort is made to *save everyone*, so very few are put into Group Three. I'm sure that in the case of a major terrorist attack, however, the Group Three designation will be widely used again.

After a couple of months, I was no longer a newbie. It's in the nature of the military that people leave on a regular basis (DEROS or maybe killed), and then are replaced. I was making rounds with this new surgeon. He was all excited. He had been in country for only a few days, and already he'd made a discovery that was worth a publication in a major medical journal.

"Look," he said. "My patient, this eighty-year-old Vietnamese woman, is twenty-four hours post-op appendectomy. Remarkably, she has required no narcotics at all. All she does is smoke her marijuana. Nowhere in the literature does it state that marijuana has analgesic properties. I'm going to sit down and write a letter to the New England Journal of Medicine. I think this is worth a publication, and I think we will have to legalize marijuana for its remarkable analgesic qualities."

I gently educated him to the fact that the joints available in Vietnam are almost universally adulterated with heroin. Heroin makes a fine analgesic, but I don't think heroin is about to be legalized anytime soon.

Humor alleviated the boredom, but laughter never lasted long. There was always an incident to bring us back to the horrors of war.

On one occasion, a bunch of soldiers arrived, and all were missing arms and legs. We were unprepared to receive all these casualties at once. It was chaos. "What happened?" I asked one the guys. It seems that they were scheduled to DEROS (Date of Expected Return from Over Seas, or something like that) back to the states the next day. The powers that be decided to be efficient, and they collected all of their weapons a bit too early. They left them only their .45s. Naturally, they were overrun that night and massacred.

Twenty years later, I visited the Vietnam memorial, and when I walked along that black wall in Washington, I thought about the terrible toll that war takes. I thought back to that day in the ER when I saw all those boys on the stretchers, without arms and legs, and I could not understand what they had accomplished with their awful sacrifice. Did Kennedy, Johnson, or Nixon realize the real cost of their "political" decisions? I could see from the teary eyes around me at the wall that the other visitors felt the same. Man's inhumanity to man, however, was never so clear to me than the night we received those casualties. I don't recall the number, but I remembered that they saturated our little medical facility. I will not attempt to describe here the terrible waste of life that I witnessed.

CHAPTER IV

I HAVE TO VENT!

My personal feelings are that the Vietnamese army lacked the willingness to fight and die for their country. I suspect that the problem, from the beginning, was that the South really didn't have a choice between communism and democracy, but a choice between communism and Prime Minister Ngo Diem's dictatorial government. The South Vietnamese enjoyed competent politics only for the short time that President Ky was in power. Otherwise, from top to bottom the government ran on graft and corruption, keeping the average Vietnamese destitute. Not much to die for.

I was in Vietnam in 1969 and 1970. In 1968, President Johnson had chosen not to run for re-election. He left office with "Hey! Hey! LBJ. How many babies did you kill today?" echoing in his ears. Nixon was elected President. The American people were disillusioned. We were now in the longest war in the history of our country. At Harvard, students protested against the university's Reserve Officers' Training Program.

Soon after I arrived in Vietnam, Nixon began pulling out troops, and he planned to end the war within a year. This was not fast enough for many Americans. In May of 1970, we were still bombing North Vietnam. The students protested at Kent State University and four students were killed, two boys and two girls.

The American people became bitter, and our government lost their support. In 1992 when Clinton ran for president, the fact that he was a draft dodger was only mentioned in passing. The average voter had not served in the military, and after Vietnam would probably have run to Canada to avoid service. Many of the 1992 voters were children at the time of Vietnam, and to talk about Vietnam made as much sense as the ancient history of World War II, or the Peloponnesian war. Many of our government officials had avoided service in Vietnam, even though they were of age. We all remember the "war records" of Clinton's and Dan Quayle but how many know that Newt Gingrich, Trent Lott, and Dick Cheney never saw action either? The elder George H. Bush was a World War II war hero, but George W. Bush joined the Air National Guard in the 1960s, and thereby avoided combat.

Contrast this with our earlier presidents. Franklin D. Roosevelt was 4F because of his polio history, but he came from a whole family of soldiers. We've all heard of Teddy and the charge at San Juan. Truman was captain of an artillery unit in the First World War (he had to lie about his age to get in), Eisenhower had five stars, Kennedy captained a World War II Torpedo Boat, and Carter graduated from Annapolis and served in the Navy. From the beginning of our country, most of our presidents have served. There has always been a conflict regarding the armed services. Our first president was the General of the Revolutionary Army, and then we had the War of 1812, the war with Mexico, and we also had our Indian wars and the Civil War.

It makes me uncomfortable to think that somebody could attain the highest rank in the military, that of Commander-in-Chief, have the power to determine when we send men and women to fight and die, and yet never have served at a lower rank. It's almost as crazy as me entering the service as a Captain.

I don't feel that service in the military automatically qualifies you for a political position. And military service doesn't guarantee you'll win the Presidency. Look at John McCain. Serving in Vietnam, spending years in a POW camp, and refusing release until your buddies are released, shows strength of character that is invaluable in a public servant. To me, it is remarkable how poorly Senator McCain, with such a remarkable record, did against

George W. in the run for the 2000 Republican ticket. I guess money speaks loudly.

What a confusing mess. Did we have any business in Vietnam? Were we really preventing the enslavement of a people by this ogre, Communism, or were we supporting a dictatorship that was doing a pretty good job of enslaving their people? Was it really an unwinnable war, or just unwinnable with the restrictions we placed upon ourselves? Did we win after all? Southeast Asia today seems to be drifting slowly toward capitalism anyway. They just don't have free elections – yet.

Napoleon conquered Europe and gave his relatives the job of governing his various conquests. At the end, his relatives proved to be poor politicians. The gains were lost, and Europe essentially returned to its pre-Napoleonic state. Napoleon's only lasting mark on this world was his Napoleonic Law. All that war and all that killing, and nothing is changed. In the same way, I wonder if it really made much difference who won the war in Vietnam. If we won, we would have eventually come to terms with the Communists. Just as today, one of our great allies is Japan, an old enemy. Today, even with the Communists as victors, there is movement toward capitalism, and old enemies are becoming friends.

In 1969, at the 71st Evac we were well aware that the war was winding down, and that we were in the midst of a massive troop withdrawal. We began to salivate. Many of us expressed the thought that "Maybe I won't have to stay here the entire 365 days after all. Maybe I'll be part of the next troop withdrawal."

The army didn't seem to work that way. They didn't send lots of soldiers home early. It appears that all they did was send in no replacements for the guys who reached DEROS. They allowed attrition to decrease our representation in Vietnam. Nobody I knew got to go home before the magic 365 days. That is, with one exception. His name was Hawkeye, and we will meet him in Cam Ranh.

Nixon sent a secret letter to Ho Chi Minh asking for serious negotiations to end the war. However, in November 1969, the full details of the My Lai massacre were made public, and in December Nixon announced a fourth American troop withdrawal. The North Vietnamese had access to television sets, and they could see that the war was ripping America apart. The unilateral withdrawal of American troops cinched it. The North Vietnamese realized that they had the upper hand, and there was no need for negotiations. They were going to have a total victory, and all that was required was a little patience.

The docs and nurses talked about what we were doing here. Was it worth it? I think I was in the majority when I said that I felt that we were in Vietnam on a noble mission. We were here to save a people's freedom. I pictured a giant monolithic political entity called "Communism." This entity was out to enslave the world. Vietnam was one domino in a series of dominos in the Pacific. Unfortunately, I was sucked into this line of thinking just like the Defense Secretary, McNamara.

Some were not so naïve. The Chief of Surgery bitterly said, "This hole is not worth an American soldier's life, not one single American arm or leg." The chief had seen a lot more blood and guts than I had.

Another doc tried to get me interested in some books on the history of Vietnam. He tried to convince me that the United States had not been straight and above board over the years, and that the North Vietnamese had some legitimate complaints. I wouldn't listen as I was thoroughly indoctrinated.

After coming home, I picked up a few books on the history of Vietnam. I'm sort of a liberal Republican. I would vote Democrat, but the party has never presented us with another Harry Truman, so I end up voting Republican in each election. Then, I shared the fear of Communism, like many Republicans, but now I can accept the fact that our overwhelming fear of communism actually prolonged a country's agony as it fought for independence. I tend to kick myself around the block for being so naive, but I keep reminding myself that I didn't have my retrospectroscope with me at the time. It's a mythical medical instrument that allows you to look into the future so that you don't do something dumb in the present. The trouble is that nobody has such an instrument. We are all mortal. Doctors make mistakes no matter how careful they are, especially when viewed through the wonderful rectrospectroscope. We have to allow the same error for politicians. I know that a doctor's error may mean a life, and a politician's error may involve millions of lives, but God makes the rules.

I'm left with a taste of bitterness. I served my country, but essentially wasted a couple of years in a fruitless pursuit due to bad judgment from a bunch of politicians. I could have used the years for some additional training in my specialty, and the little medicine that I practiced in Vietnam had little effect in the whole scheme of things. In the great summation, we ended many lives, and damaged many others with little accomplished.

CHAPTER 5

THE MIDDLE OF NOWHERE

Pleiku was situated on a high plateau in the middle of a dense, triple-canopied jungle. It was triple-canopied because it had three roofs. The short vegetation was tall enough to reach over your head, and came together over your head to block the sun. Above that the branches of the tall trees met overhead to form a second roof. Between these two canopies, middle-size vegetation formed another roof.

From the beginning you knew that you were in the middle of nowhere. You just had to look over this vast vista of solid green to realize that you were totally isolated from the "real world." If it weren't for the friends you made in this strange place, you would probably go totally nuts. Your immediate community was isolated and small. Its border was demarcated by barbed wire, and only about the area of a large city block. You ended up knowing everyone on the block, and you made some pretty close friends. We had very little to occupy ourselves except these friendships.

Entertainment during leisure hours was limited. Boredom was oppressive. About once a week we watched a --16mm movie in the mess. Except for a few drinks at the Officers' Club, that was it. One of my buddies in Cam Ranh used his spare time to learn to ride a unicycle. Somewhere in the city of Cam Ranh, he had found somebody to sell him a one-wheeled bike.

In the first couple of weeks, the nights were particularly difficult. I would leave the mess after a movie, and walk down a dark path toward my hootch. Since all the windows were covered to block the lights, I would invariably wander off in the wrong direction. Sometimes I'd fall into a ditch. It sounds funny now, but at the time it just made me feel isolated and at risk. After a few weeks, I had the steps memorized and could find my way home like a blind man.

Then there was the smell. Boy, was it foul, and closing the window offered little protection. "What is this awful stuff I smell?" I asked this veteran.

"Oh, that's Nuoc mam," he responded. "It is made by stacking dead fish on a mat of tree limbs. The fish are allowed to rot in the sun, and the oil that drains is collected. Supposedly, it makes a great tasting sauce. It's a real delicacy for the Vietnamese."

"Have you ever tasted it?" I asked.

"No! As you can see, a Westerner can't get close enough to take a taste. The odor is too overpowering."

Our tastes and prejudices are governed by our society. We had local people take care of the housekeeping at the base. The officers had women who did their laundry and swept out the hootch. Naturally, we called them "hootch maids." Periodically, my hootch maid would bring in some food from home, and insist that I try it. I usually found the dishes quite tasty, but she almost always refused to identify the ingredients. The doctors on the base decided to give the hootch maids a taste of real American cooking. We got some great steaks from the Air Force PX, and set up a barbecue. To our surprise, the hootch maids found the beef distasteful, and a few even refused to taste the meat. It was too foreign to their taste buds. Just as foreign as Nuoc mam was to our taste buds.

On rare occasions, someone would bring entertainment to the Officer's Club. These little diversions were welcomed, but I never saw the likes of somebody like Bob Hope. Most of the entertainers were Vietnamese. They played music like *Leaving on a Jet Plane,* or *Blowing in the Wind.* It's funny how many songs in the Sixties were about being away from home. I don't usually get flashbacks, but when I hear that music today, my eyes tear up, and some of those memories come flooding in.

The highlands had monsoon seasons. Monsoons were supposed to hit only twice a year, once in mid-May, and once in November. But in reality they last about four months. I swear, I went through two monsoons during the six months I was in Pleiku. That means it rained every day. In the morning we would have a rain. There was no lightning, and no wind, just a downpour like somebody had opened the gates at the Hoover Dam. Forget raindrops—this was a solid torrent of water. By afternoon, it was as if somebody turned off a giant spigot: the rain would suddenly stop. Then the sun would shine, and you couldn't find a cloud in the sky. Since we were on a mountain, the water ran off, and the ground would quickly dry. Then the next day it would hit us again.

During the cold season, I often slept in my clothes since the hootch wasn't heated. I doubt that the temperature ever dropped below 55 degrees, even at night, but for a Florida boy, that's pretty uncomfortable. Finally, I got the bright idea to order an electric heater from Sears. It took a while for it to arrive in Vietnam, and I didn't receive it until I'd been transferred to Cam Rahn Bay. Great timing! The temperature never drops below 90 in Cam Rahn.

Nurses! Ah, the nurses! I bet you picture Hot Lips in *M*A*S*H*,* or those gorgeous creatures in *China Beach.* Actually, some of the women were very attractive, which we could really appreciate when they wore their Bikinis. Yes, we had a small swimming pool at the 71st Evac in Pleiku. Later, at the 6th Convalescent Center in Cam Rahn we didn't have a pool, but there was a magnificent beach, allowing us to ogle the nurses on the sand. At all other times, the nurses were dressed in baggy combat fatigues that were not only excellent when you wanted to hide in the jungle, but also hid any hint of the shape of the person inside them. When gathered in groups of three or more, even the prettiest nurses appeared to be a herd of elephants or rhinoceros in heavy combat boots with steel soles. This was perfect for stomping to death any Vietcong that dared to approach.

The Air Force was worse. The women wore balloon-like baggy pants, which were so ugly it was hard not to laugh when any of them approached.

In spite of the tremendous ratio of one woman among thousands, the nurses were treated with the greatest respect. We couldn't help ogling them because of the scarcity of available women, but they had their privacy, and were made as comfortable as possible in a tough situation. They were all officers; the lowest rank among the nurses was second lieutenant, so they were respectfully addressed as "yes Ma'am," or "no Ma'am" by the grunts.

Unfortunately, there were also male nurses. There's nothing wrong with male nurses. It's just that there was a ratio of about one woman for every ten thousand men in the area, and we could always use a few more women.

In the army, a nurse's working day is not just eight hours, it's twelve hours. They work hard. Nurses all over the world get used to seeing the dying. What is the profession of nursing, but to take care of the ill, the aged, those near death? But nursing in Vietnam was different. Here you took care of boys, many as young as eighteen. They cared for them as they died. Sometimes they helped them write their last letter home, saying their good-byes. They comforted them when they discovered their loss of limbs, eyes, and penises. A combat-experienced veteran develops this 1000-yard stare. After a while, you would see the same look in the eyes of many a nurse.

I didn't work that hard. In fact, I faced hours of boredom. I came in as a Captain, a Captain out of the chain of command who had no leadership responsibilities. I was just a doctor. Three months later, they made me a Major. No change here either, just a slight increase in pay. Some of the regular army types were bitter about this. Imagine the struggle of making it through West Point, and going in as a second lieutenant. At this point, you see many of your friends die. The mortality rate of second lieutenants is extremely high. The road from second lieutenant, to first and then to captain is a tough one. Many of those who survive combat wash out before they make it. Now, you meet somebody who never took a course related to the military, doesn't even know how to salute properly, and he's a Captain or even a Major. This guy doesn't know SAM from Spam, and you're expected to be the first to execute the salute since he is your superior.. He, on the other hand, has to answer the salute out of courtesy in recognition of your inferior rank.

Believing that a higher rank merely means more money, more responsibility, and more ego, the average civilian does not appreciate how important it is to advance in rank. Imagine the mail clerk who's been in the company for twenty years. He started as a mail clerk who never had ambition, and now he's ready to retire. The armed services don't work that way. You don't get to stay a second lieutenant, or any other rank. You have just so many years to advance to the next grade. If you don't make it, you are washed out of the army. They need your space for the people moving up, and you in turn must keep moving up. If you don't, you're out. If you want a military career, this can be a great blow.

One major barrier to advancement is the fact that there are more second lieutenants than first lieutenants, more first lieutenants than captains, and more captains than majors. Finally you get to a mere handful of general officers. This is a murderous pyramid system. It's obvious that somebody has to leave at each stage, and you fight like the dickens to keep it from being you. You must manage to stay in this rat race at least twenty years. If you survive only nineteen years and eleven months, you don't get retirement pay. The army career is not a soft job.

People get old and infirm in the Army, too. I've seen men become disabled from disease just before their twenty-year stint is up. If you can't work, out you go. There are younger, healthier guys waiting for your job. Oh, you were tossed out three weeks before retirement? Too bad, no retirement pay for you.

I remember hiding an old sergeant's medical record for weeks when I was at my duty station at Fort Jackson. The lack of his medical record was the only thing that stalled his paper work, and kept this guy from being fired. I was roundly criticized, since it didn't take long for command to figure out what was happening. Nobody guaranteed you a rose garden in the Army, and if you became disabled, that's life. Being an "obligate volunteer," and not regular Army, I had no second thoughts about sliding his file behind a drawer.

Doctors, cooks, engineers, and mail clerks were all members of the "support group." Only one soldier in five was a combatant. Our major enemy was not the North Vietnamese, it was boredom. Guitars are relatively portable, compared to pianos (you can't throw your piano over your shoulder when you're called to another duty station, and a baby grand doesn't fit in a Huey very well). Many of my buddies were trying to teach themselves to play harmonicas or guitars.

Musical instruments did not interest me at the moment, and I needed something else to fill up my spare time. I discovered that some of the nurses were studying Tae Kwon Do from a Korean, and I was invited to try a few classes. At the time I wasn't interested. Here I was, in the country where Tae Kwon Do is the national sport, and I missed my chance to study from one of the natives. I'm still kicking myself around the block for missing this opportunity. I was younger at the time, and not too old to improve my skills and my flexibility. Later, at the age of 48, I discovered that I enjoyed the martial arts, but by that time age had calcified my tendons, and my joint mobility. Today, even though I'm a black belt, it is a major effort to try not to look like a total incompetent at the dojang.

One day I saw a nurse running laps just inside of the perimeter on a dirt road that followed the barbed wire surrounding the compound. It couldn't have been more than a mile around. I'd been going nuts trying to figure out what to do with my spare time. I thought, "What a great idea." So I started to run. The course was limited to the road just within the perimeter. Outside the perimeter was Charlie's land, and I wasn't interested in bumping into him.

I guess this was one of the important things that I got out of Vietnam. Until that moment, I'd been a slob, a couch potato. I gained weight in medical school. Now I had something to do. Vietnam turned me into a long distance runner. A few years later, I ran the Orange Bowl Marathon in Miami. I didn't break any records, but I made the 26 miles. Forty two years after Vietnam, I'm still in shape. I don't run distance any longer, but I'm in the martial arts, and have made 3rd dan in Tae Kwon Do. I never could have accomplished this if I hadn't started endurance training when I was in Pleiku.

CHAPTER 6

STILL NO URINE

I'm not a surgeon, I'm an internist. I do not cut. Oh, I would occasionally assist in the operating room, but this would be limited to hanging onto a retractor. Once, when I was assisting in surgery on a Vietnamese with appendicitis, the surgeon turned toward me and handed me the scalpel. This was Vietnam, with no hospital review committees asking why an internist was doing general surgery. I was a bit tempted, but I knew I lacked a whole encyclopedia of training. Politely declining, I didn't know the first thing about cutting. I returned the scalpel to the surgeon, and went back to holding the retractor.

I treated hundreds of cases of Malaria. I became an expert on Malaria. The average doctor knows next to nothing about Malaria. He thinks you can find the parasite on a random blood smear. He has no idea that it may take days of hunting, the taking of many blood samples, and finally may even require a bone marrow sample. A high spiking fever is a non-specific sign. Too many other diseases, such as Dengue, give you the same fever. Treatment is also not straightforward. We have several kinds of Malaria, and much of it has become resistant to the common drugs.

Since my return to the real world, I have seen only one case in thirty years. In Vietnam, I also saw hundreds of cases of hepatitis and a few cases of typhus. The other prominent disease was heroin addiction, but more about that later.

The heat and dehydration also played tricks on the soldiers. A grunt was sent to the evac complaining of severe back pain. He knew he was very ill since he hadn't peed for hours. We poured fluid into him. Still no urine. Then we went another direction. We gave him massive doses of Lasix, a very powerful diuretic, but still no urine. The back pain made us think of a kidney stone, but if you completely blocked up one kidney, you still should be making urine from the other kidney. The commander accused us of using too much Lasix. He said, "You're going to burst his kidneys." Of course, that's nonsense. You can't do that with Lasix, but the commander was a surgeon, and cannot be expected to know much beyond carpentry.

Finally, I called the Field Hospital in Saigon. This hospital was the Mecca of medicine in Vietnam, the Southeast Asian version of Massachusetts General. I told him that we had an anuric GI, and didn't have the foggiest idea what was going on. I hopped on a helicopter, transferred to a C130 and accompanied the patient to the Saigon Army Hospital.

A week later, I called to get a follow-up. What was wrong with my patient? He had a problem that I'd never seen back in CONUS. As it turned out, his dehydration was so severe that he developed stones in both kidneys. The stones rolled into both ureters and blocked the flow from both kidneys simultaneously.

We would occasionally take a ride to far off towns to offer our services. In one of these small cities, Kon Tum, an American civilian doctor ran a small hospital. Doctor Pat Smith was a legend. The administrator and the doctor in this little hospital, Pat Smith was a civilian who volunteered to go to Vietnam, and she did not have the security of being part of an army facility. Periodically, the Vietcong would sweep through, killing and raping her patients while she and the staff hid in closets. Then, she and the surviving staff would come out and start all over again. We would visit, but before nightfall we returned to the comfort and security of our base.

Doctor Pat Smith's M.D. was from University of Washington. She moved to Kontum in the late 1950s. She remained there for 13 years, and became known as the ya pogang tih, or Big Mother of Medicine. At the end of the war she returned to Seattle. She planned to return to the Central Highlands, but never made it. She died at the age of 78 in the United States. She is survived by Vietnamese children she adopted while at her hospital in Kontum.

She is still fondly remembered. I once signed onto an Internet newsletter for Vietnam veterans. Some of them were still asking, "What ever happened to Pat Smith?"

The International Catholic Relief was her sponsor. If anybody deserves the title of "Saint," she certainly does.

On my first visit to Pat Smith's hospital, my commander pointed out that the patients' beds were merely a few wood planks supported by concrete blocks. Only a thin blanket separated their skin from the wood.

"Look at that," the colonel exclaimed. "Look how they have to live, and do you hear any complaints?"

I looked up at him. "Maybe we don't hear any complaints because we don't understand their language." I responded.

Getting there was most exciting. We would use a group of helicopters called Hueys, the UH-1 helicopter used for medical evacuation. The biggest and fastest roller coaster can't hold a candle to this mode of transportation. The sides of the helicopter held big barn doors that stayed open in flight. I sat on the floor with my feet hanging outside. A safety belt was passed around my waist. Then it was latched to a ringbolt in the deck so that even though the pilot banked the helicopter sharply, my tether would keep me from sliding out the door.

A helicopter flies through enemy territory by either of two techniques. The first method is to fly at an altitude of many thousand feet, beyond the reach of small arms fire. Sitting on the floor, with your feet dangling, is akin to sitting on a top ledge of the Empire State Building, a real thrill if you like that sort of thing. The other mode of travel is to fly just a couple of feet off a highway. The helicopter would rise a few feet now and then, to let a car pass below. Although the chopper is in range of small arms fire, nobody could aim and shoot as the helicopter zipped pass. This was the ultimate roller coaster ride.

Several presidents have exclaimed upon leaving office that what they miss the most are those helicopter rides. They rarely mention Air Force One.

One of my patients told me an interesting helicopter experience. He jumped aboard one night, and wrapped the restraining strap around his waist, intending to hook it into the ring in the deck. He missed the ring as the helicopter rose and banked away. He slid out the open door and into the darkness. He estimated that the altitude was at least fifty feet. Hoping for a quick and merciful death, he fell though the darkness and landed in a canal just below him. He wasn't injured, but his entire life history passed before him.

Forget about idle conversation in a helicopter. Just as in the C130 cargo plane, the engine noise was deafening. You couldn't talk to your buddy, even at a yell. I'm sure the pilots had some sort of microphone/earphone system buried in their helmets, otherwise the crew couldn't communicate.

At high altitude, I'd look down at the endless jungle below. Occasionally, I'd see jungle pockmarked with giant discs of bare earth. These were the sites of B52 strikes. Each massive bomb — called a cookie cutter—would leave a giant crater in the earth. The bombs were designed to be dropped in the jungle where they would clear a large circle. This cleared area could then be used as a LZ (landing zone) for helicopters. However, they were often used against personnel. These gigantic, destructive weapons were totally demoralizing to the North. The noise and vibration from one of those monsters must have been horrendous.

It is impossible to conceive of the tremendous tonnage of bombs and other ordinance dropped in Southeast Asia during the Vietnam war. It is estimated that we delivered to this relatively small area about 7,500,000 tons and thus about three times the weight used by the Allies in the Second World War – Pacific and European theaters combined.

Many experts felt that airpower used in this way in Vietnam was futile. In the Second World War we bombed strategically. We destroyed factories, sources of fuel, etc. We forced Germany to move factories into the country side and greatly reduced their efficiency.

Bombing civilian targets has proven ineffective. The Blitz, during World War Two, merely angered the British people and united them into a common cause. One of Hitler's major errors was to have used his bombs against civilian targets. They would have been much more effectively used against Britain's radar and airfields. The English pilots took the Luftwaffe apart during Britain's "Finest Hour." You see, the English had invented radar.

We could not use our air power in a strategic sense. The source of production was in North Vietnam. We were not allowed to strike their factories or destroy their ports. I believe that by limiting our targets we affected morale and assured our lack of success.

These giant craters reminded me of what was really happening. There were American soldiers down there. Many were dropped by helicopter miles from civilization, expecting to get blown away at every turn in the jungle.

Some soldiers stepped on Bouncing Betties, land mines that were not intended to kill. When triggered, they would pop up waist high, and blow genitals to pieces. They were meant to maim and demoralize, and they served their purpose well.

Hidden in the high grass along the side of the path were sharpened bamboo punji sticks, covered with human excrement. The PAVN would start shooting. The natural response would be to dive for cover at the side of the path. And you would be impaled on one of these spears. A puncture from a punji stick rarely killed immediately. The purpose, of course, was to cause injury, then infection, and only much later, death. Meanwhile, the grunt would become a burden upon his buddies, slow their progress, and in general, interfere with the mission.

When I resigned my commission with the Army, I purchased an album of songs written by Vietnam veterans. The surprising thing was that half of the songs were not about the hardships of being a GI in Vietnam. Their subject was the war as seen by the Vietcong. As terrible as the American GI's experience had been, it didn't compare with that of the North Vietnamese. Imagine that you have no air cover. Yet you must drive your truck down a jungle trail. You may even be chained to the seat of your vehicle. You cannot call in artillery when you're attacked. There is no artillery, just as there are no friendly airplanes. They had one million deaths, while we suffered 58,000. There is nothing for the North Vietnamese to do but to pray when the American B52s start dropping their bombs.

We did our best medically to serve the communities around us. This was not exactly a safe exercise. On one occasion, a doctor was attending a line of Vietnamese, handing out the usual ointments and antibiotics. The next in line was a ten-year-old boy. Suddenly the marine standing next to the doc, pulled out his sidearm and killed the boy. The boy had been hiding a .45 behind his back.

We knew that after we performed our bit of modern medicine and then left, the town was back in the 16th century. I'm sure that nothing we did had any lasting effect, with one exception. I believe that our medical assistance, in the villages, was part of the American war policy to befriend the civilian. We didn't care, it made us feel good that we might be doing something of value among all the bad stuff.

There was an ophthalmologist at the 71st Evac who took a Montagnard on as an apprentice. A Montagnard doesn't speak a written language, and every tribe has a different dialect or language. I'm sure you've never heard of their languages. They speak Bahnar, Mnong, Sedang, Jarai, Roglai, or Rade. Therefore, getting an interpreter is almost impossible. Their leader is usually a shaman.

The ophthalmologist taught this Montagnard to perform cataract surgery. Did he understand pathophysiology? Could he handle a post op complication? Was he that great in making a diagnosis? He probably got an "F" in all of those areas. But he learned to recognize a dense cataract, and more important, to fix it. When this ophthalmologist left Vietnam, he left something of lasting value.

The Montagnards were our allies, and we supplied them with medical care. They lived in a world "lighted by fire," living by campfires in absolute primitive living conditions. Yet, when necessary, they entered the confines of the steel bird. They entered the helicopter, having complete trust in their friends. They relied heavily on a crossbow, designed to fire a pointed stick whose point was hardened by a fire treatment. It had no steel or flint arrowhead. Like many of my friends, I followed the crowd and bought one.

Beautifully inlaid with ivory, it was otherwise a crude device. It took all my strength to stretch the cord across the trigger mechanism. I had to try it out. I placed one of those sharpened sticks in the bow, and aimed at my door. The door was solid, hard wood. Not one of those hollow things we have in CONUS. The arrow was driven about ½" into the wood. This thing deserved some respect.

I had several Montagnard patients. One Montagnard was in renal failure due to Malaria. This is called black water fever because the byproducts of blood in the urine colored the urine black. If you can kill the Malaria parasite, and keep the patient alive long enough, the kidneys will heal. To keep him alive I had to take over the job of his kidneys--I had to dialyze him, and the only means we had was called peritoneal dialysis. I injected a local anesthetic into the skin of his abdomen, and then used a giant needle called a trocar (this needle is the size of a railroad spike). By twisting it I was able to work its way through the abdominal wall. In this way we could run large volume of fluids in and out of his abdomen, and use his gut as a makeshift kidney membrane. Clean water would pass into his abdomen, and water with dissolved metabolic byproducts (toxins) would be washed out.

During this procedure, he calmly watched me twist and push that trocar into his abdomen without any complaint. There was no need to restrain him. He was entirely trusting.

A couple of days later, he was visited by several family members. This time they were able to find an interpreter. They finally made me understand that they wanted to take my patient home.

"But he is in kidney failure. Without dialysis, he will die."

"But we must take him home. Our witch doctor wants to take over his care."

"No problem," I responded. "He can care for him here in the hospital. I will arrange for one case hospital privileges."

Their doctor came, and I watched from the door as he made his incantations and shook his gourds. The patient had attention from his "primary care physician," and I was able to continue with his dialysis. With our combined care, his kidneys healed, and I was able to discharge him home. End of case.

My time was not totally consumed by my official duties. I was able to get away, at times, to explore the surrounding country. I once came upon a hospital staffed only by nurses. This was a civilian Vietnamese hospital and lacked the luxuries we see in hospitals back in the states. There were no doctors on the staff, and the staff was all Vietnamese. A nurse begged me to make rounds. "Why?" I asked.

"Unless you make rounds, we can't discharge any of our patients. That is one of the rules." She pleaded. The hospital was completely full.

She explained that they had rules: The nurses could admit a patient, but the patient could not be discharged before being examined by some itinerant doctor. I was the itinerant doctor.

"Who writes the orders when a patient is admitted?" I asked.

I found out that it was the nurses who wrote the orders. In the United States, the doctor writes the orders, and the nurse carries them out. Here they were doing double duty. They were actually writing their own orders.

Suppose a patient presented with a fever? You couldn't expect the average nurse to be an expert diagnostician. So every patient would automatically get ten lines of orders that included the following regimen:

1. Penicillin just in case it was a bacterial infection.
2. Isoniazid, just in case it was tuberculosis.
3. Quinine, since Malaria was quite popular.
4. Aspirin to control fever.
5. Cortisone just in case it was not an infection, but some other inflammatory problem.

Numbers 6,7,8,9, and 10 were five other drugs that I don't recall, but covered all of the other possibilities.

You don't need to have medical training to realize that this was not the best of medicine. I had to remind myself that many small towns in the United States have no physicians. The shortage in Vietnam was much more severe than ours in CONUS, and in addition, there was a war on. Getting an ambulance to take you to the nearest major city was just not practical.

One of the patients I saw in this hospital was a young girl of about sixteen who was dying of starvation. She was psychologically traumatized, as was everybody else in Vietnam.

She would not eat. To me this was a typical case of anorexia nervosa. We have many teenagers in CONUS who die of this disease. In CONUS, the teenager wants to be thin and beautiful, and then develops a strange disorder of body concept. You might see her as a bundle of skin and bones. She looks in the mirror and sees a morbidly obese girl. Finally, she can never be thin enough and ends up killing herself by starvation. When I was in training, back in the sixties, we were told to treat this disease by force-feeding. By passing a feeding tube through the nose and into the stomach, the patient would finally realize that resistance was futile, and start eating on her own. So I passed a feeding tube, and instructed the nurses in her tube feeding.

The next day I returned, and found that the tube had been removed. "Why?" I asked a nurse. The nurse responded that there were too many people dying who wanted to live. They didn't have time to waste on somebody who didn't want to live.

There is no doubt that the Vietnamese nurses had a much stronger union than the army nurses. Our nurses worked 12-hour shifts, and our patients were cared for 24 hours a day, seven days a week, 52 weeks per year. If a nurse was disabled, another nurse would double her shift. A typical American nurse will not abandon the floor until she is relieved or collapses from exhaustion.

"So what?" you say. "Isn't that the way things have always been?"

The Vietnamese nurse goes home at 5pm. She takes the weekend and holidays off. There are no nurses in the hospital after 5 PM, or Friday night through Monday morning.

"Wait a minute," you say. "The Tet holiday is about 10 days long. Who feeds, and cares for the patients?"

The family must come in and care for the patient. If there is no family, the patient is in big trouble. We once had a Vietnamese patient at the 71st Evac who was to be transferred to a local Vietnamese hospital. We were warned to be sure that the patient arrived before 5pm. Our helicopter crew dropped the patient off on the helicopter pad late Friday, and flew off. The pilot was a bit uncomfortable about that, so Sunday evening they took a fly by the hospital. Sure enough, the patient was still lying next to the helicopter-landing pad.

I also came across one of the Vietnamese community hospitals, which were nothing more than a few open lean-tos. The patients were lying on blankets, directly on the ground. Except for the lean-to roof, the patient was exposed to the elements. I was approached by the lab tech. He was a Vietnamese dressed in rags. He reminded me of Gandhi. He told me that he had a patient who he suspected of having tuberculosis of the central nervous system. He needed to examine some spinal fluid, but there were no doctors and no spinal needles in the hospital.

The only needle available was a regular 20 gage 1 ½ inch needle. I squatted in the dirt beside the patient. I laid him on his side, and I had him hug his knees to his chest. I used the needle to enter the spinal canal. I presented the lab tech with a few drops of spinal fluid. I figured that he must have a microscope stashed under a bush somewhere, and just wanted to examine the fluid for bacteria.

"Is that all you got?" He looked at me as if I was an idiot. "With these few drops, how can I check the sugar, and protein? How can I do a colloidal gold test?"

I had seriously misjudged the place. Somewhere in this group of shacks was a full service lab, and the lab tech, wearing little but rags, was highly trained.

I knew that I was going to face culture shock and loneliness. Before I left for Vietnam, I told my wife, Diane that our love was strong enough to survive a year of separation. It was also strong enough that if either one of us found another sexual partner for a while it was no big thing. I don't think she was extremely happy with the concept, but again, a year is a long time.

My hootch maid was Mai, an attractive Vietnamese woman, who had about five children. Her husband was a soldier in the South Vietnamese Army. It didn't take long for us to start our sexual relationship. When I say that this was strictly a sexual relationship, I am not exaggerating. I could speak only a few words of Vietnamese, words like pain. She could speak some English, but it was simple English. We could not discuss feelings, our philosophy about the war, or much of anything else. In short, all we could do was to express our immediate needs. Her husband was away fighting in the jungle somewhere, my wife was back home in CONUS and we were both cut off from sex with our spouses. The opportunity was there and it seemed like the natural thing. (Plate X).

My wife and I understood that one year of separation would seem like a century. We didn't have an "open" marriage, but a bit of straying, on either part, would not affect our relationship. I never asked Diane if she formed any liaisons when I was gone. I don't have that kind of curiosity, and unlike most people, I don't feel it should be a major factor in a marriage – certainly when you've been gone a whole year.

A couple of times she invited me to visit her at her home. She kept telling me that her husband wouldn't mind, and he was away, anyway. I didn't feel comfortable going into this little village with all her children. Besides, maybe her husband would come home. Maybe he would mind a lot. Maybe he belonged to the Vietcong. Maybe he would slit my throat.

In that little village, I would have absolutely no security, and except for the barb wire enclosing the perimeter, the Vietcong owned the countryside at night.

I learned that many of the women had large families. Contraception was a complete mystery to them. I bought my condoms at the PX, but for the Vietnamese, many of whom were Catholic, there was no access to contraceptives. I asked the Vietnamese staff about birth control pills. They didn't know what I was talking about. They had been kept in complete ignorance of the major factor that had meant sexual freedom for the rest of the world.

I would get a care package from home every few weeks. My sisters had a sense of humor, and always threw in a few "delicacies." I got bottles of fried ants, and chocolate covered bees. I wrote to Diane, and asked her to raid the "sample room" at the health department, where she now worked. She was to toss in a few boxes of birth control pills with the cookies and other goodies that I received in my care package. I planned to distribute the birth control pills to the Vietnamese women who worked on the base.

The package came. It had obviously been opened, and although the cake and cookies were intact, there were no birth control pills. I suspect that the sex police had confiscated them.

Mai was doing the housework around the hootch when I noticed that her hands were stained black. "What's the black stuff?" I asked.

"Oh, that's black hair dye."

Vietnamese have natural coal black hair, so the hair dye made no sense at all. "But, your hair is pitch black. Why the hair dye?"

"All the Vietnamese women dye their hair. We are afraid that if there is just a hint of brown, the others will think that we are not pure Vietnamese. They will think that perhaps our father had been in the French Army, and that we have French blood. That would be number ten."

The Vietnamese had an interesting way of expressing whether something was good or bad. If it was "number ten," it was very bad. If it was "number one," it was the best. I never heard anybody rate anything a "seven" or a "three."

The hootch maids were allowed to work in the compound, but at a price. They were not trusted. Every time they left for the evening, they were subjected to a search. This often included a body cavity search by rubber-gloved MPs. We felt that many would steal, and we knew that many had connections with the other side. The process of waiting in line for somebody to grope inside of you must have been particularly demeaning, but these people needed the work or their families would starve. Many of the Vietnamese hated us, as their sentiments lay with the North, but I'm sure that many of them also hated us for the way we had to treat them. I believe that many were just realistic. They may have felt that we were their friends, but they were at the mercy of the Vietcong. If the Vietcong suspected that they were truly loyal to the United States, they would wake up dead in the morning. There were many instances where village leaders were assassinated when they did not cooperate with the Vietcong. Let's not be judgmental. There were also stories regarding our assassinating village leaders who were too friendly to the other side. The Vietnamese people were the real victims in this war.

There were days when none of the Vietnamese would come to work. When that happened, we knew to expect an attack from the Vietcong. The morning would come and there would be nobody doing our laundry. The camp would be empty of

Vietnamese, and we would have this awful foreboding. I don't want to exaggerate the risks involved. The attack would consist of merely a couple of mortar rounds. It seems they just wanted us to know that they were still around. One of my buddies had a theory. They really didn't want to break anything. As I said before we had these giant radar antennas and the North knew we were leaving some day, and wanted this equipment intact.

At night we would hear the scream of Gatling guns. We assumed that the enemy was trying to penetrate our wire, and we were being protected by the helicopters. I knew they knew their job, and I felt secure. The enemy, trying to penetrate our lines, were called sappers. Their job was to "tunnel through our defense, and toss bags loaded with explosives into our buildings.

The internal medicine boards were offered in Saigon, and several of the Pleiku docs left to take them. Saigon, in turn, sent docs to the 71st Evac to cover for them. That night, I saw the newbies from Saigon, huddled in their hooches. The sound of the Gatlings caused them to fear that we were being over-run. They could not wait to get back to good, safe, Saigon. I reflected on how easy it is to get accustomed to threat. To me the Gatlings were protective and comforting.

One day Mai came to me with tears in her eyes. "I am so sad. You will be leaving me and go to Cam Ranh."

I looked at her like she was crazy. Were we having a bit of a language problem again? "What are you talking about?" I said. "I'm stationed here, period! I'm going nowhere."

"No, you go to Cam Ranh in two weeks," she insisted.

Two weeks later, I got orders to go to Cam Ranh. She knew what was coming before General Clark. Not only was I leaving the 71st Evac, but so was everyone else. One day we all stood at attention while our flag was being lowered. The 71st was being decommissioned. Oh yes, we were leaving all those communication towers that the North coveted.

I never knew of Mai's true loyalties. I suspect that all this information was obtained by spies taking care of housekeeping needs in HQ. Who knows? I could never discuss this sort of thing with her. If she was loyal to Vietcong, she would of course lie. Beyond that, I did not have enough command of Vietnamese, and she spoke little English. This allowed for sex, but not philosophical discussions.

I had a little refrigerator next to my room. I was not going to drag that thing to my next station. They certainly didn't have room in the helicopter. On the other hand, I couldn't just give it to Mai. We were not allowed to give gifts to civilians. The Army was afraid we might destroy the Vietnamese economy in some way.

As with most Vietnamese, Mai and her family had no means of keeping food cold. They had to eat the groceries they bought at the market the day of purchase. In addition to working at the base, she did her food shopping every day. They could buy ice, but that would hold food only for a short time in the tropics. Since every truck and jeep that leaves the compound is searched, how do you smuggle a refrigerator out of an army base?

A couple of my buddies loaded the refrigerator into an ambulance. We roared up to the gate and announced that we had a few stiffs in the back, and they were beginning to smell bad, and we were in a rush. We were waved right through, and we went on to her village.

She sat in the truck, and directed us to her home. There was no real road. It was just a jungle path that led us to a dirt clearing with a few chickens scratching around in the mud. The village itself consisted of a few shanties with thatched or corrugated steel roofs. Little children, dressed in a few squalid rags, peeked at us from behind walls. A couple of us lifted the refrigerator and carried it to her home. On the table was a wooden crate with ice that she had purchased at the market that morning. The makeshift icebox was how she kept her food fresh for the day. We placed the refrigerator against a wall.

I never thought to ask her if she had electricity.

That was the last time I saw Mai. After we left Vietnam, I could not help but be concerned about her fate. We were lovers, but because of language and cultural differences, we could never be in love. To be in love you must have a connection. You can't share interests if you can't understand the other person. What we shared was just pure animal lust. That's still not too bad when you're a long way from home. Yet, she was a normal, social human being. She had a family, and I met some of her friends. Now we had left, and we'd left behind somebody who was defenseless. She and many others had worked for us, and acted in support of the "occupying Army." Would the Northern forces look upon her as a traitor? What about the killing fields? This was a term used for the widespread killing of civilians in Cambodia, but could easily be applied to what happened to our Vietnamese allies when we left Vietnam. Would she end up as another pile of bones in a field, or would she be sent to a labor camp for reorientation? More than thirty years have passed, but I still think of her, and wonder about her fate. Like the man with the eyeballs on his face, some thoughts never leave you for long.

III - CAM RANH

CHAPTER 7

MY CHINA BEACH

My new assignment was the 6th Convalescent Center at Cam Ranh Bay, and it was quite a contrast. This was not actually China Beach. China Beach was a few miles north, near DaNang. Pleiku was high on a mountain; Cam Ranh Bay was at sea level. Pleiku was cool and green. Cam Ranh Bay rarely had temperatures below 100, and no green at all, just sand everywhere: sand in my hootch, sand in my hair, sand in my food, and sand in my bed. Diane sent me a letter with cookie crumbs in the envelope. I was to sprinkle the crumbs in my bed so that I would be reminded of our bed at home. I really didn't need that. I already had plenty of sand.

Some character planted a sign saying, "DO NOT WALK ON THE GRASS." I don't remember seeing a single blade. It was not uncommon for the temperature to reach 120 degrees in the shade. It wasn't as bad as it sounded, because it was a dry heat. I know this sounds like a joke, but it's an important factor. You felt as if you were walking in an oven, but the sweat would be pulled from your body, and your skin remained dry. As long as you remained hydrated, you were never too uncomfortable. I once flew from Cam Ranh to Nha Trang, where the temperature was only 85 degrees, but the humidity was close to 100%. I was in a crowded, unventilated C130. I remember sitting in the plane with my soaking wet uniform sticking to my skin, crammed shoulder to shoulder with other GIs with uniforms sticking to their skins. I couldn't wait to get back to Cam Ranh.

The Officer's Mess had air-conditioning. At least it was supposed to. The wall, where the A/C unit was installed, had a gaping hole. The air-conditioner was being repaired. In my six months at the Sixth Convalescent Center, I never got to see that A/C unit. We ate in a little dining room without even a fan. I once showed up wearing just my Army T-shirt and pants. They refused to serve me. They had a strict dress code. If I wanted to eat in the mess, I had to wear my full, long-sleeved uniform. They thought of themselves as the Brown Derby. It was unbearable to eat lunch in that get-up, in that heat.

Over the next few months, something happened to my internal thermostat. To this day I am so acclimated that I can tolerate intense heat. The martial arts gym I first went to was not air-conditioned. Occasionally in the summer, a white belt would collapse from heat exhaustion. In 95-degree, high humidity mid-summer Miami, it doesn't bother me a bit.

I was in Cam Ranh only a couple of days when I was told about a particular patient at the air base, but it was too late for my services. Now the specialist he required was a pathologist. He had arrived in Vietnam, and a few minutes later he was dead.

Most people volunteer for active duty to fight for their country. This war was different. Some of the grunts told me that many of our volunteers were heroin addicts who volunteered because they learned that all the good stuff was over here. These guys would volunteer for a second or third tour just to get our great stuff.

The heroin in the United States was only about 15% pure. In the Republic of Vietnam you could buy these little screw cap vials for about $8. Each vial contained about five grams of 100% pure heroin. This was such a great bargain that men were willing to sign up to live in dirt, and have people shoot at them, so that they could get in on it. The stuff was so pure that you didn't even need a needle. In fact, in my entire year in Vietnam, I met only one soldier who had ever used a needle with it. The user just snorted it up his nose like cocaine. That's exactly what this volunteer did. He snorted a whole cap. His buddies warned him that this was pure heroin, but he'd had plenty back at the states, and he said he could handle it. He couldn't handle it. He snorted, and immediately went into respiratory arrest and died.

When I arrived in Cam Ranh, one of the company clerks took me to my new hootch. From the outside, it looked like they had merely transplanted my home from Pleiku to this beach. I was blown away when I opened the door. I had the whole building to myself. Okay, it was only about 12 feet by 18 feet, but it was all mine. The cabin was completely paneled. What surprised me most were the well-constructed wood cabinets high on the walls. It even had a well-made bar, and a small air conditioner in the window. I actually had an air-conditioned room in Vietnam. I felt like a General.

I turned to the clerk, "This is beautiful. How come the luxury?"

Then he told me the story. The previous occupant was a Captain Hawkeye. No, I'm not making this up. That was really his nickname. The mission of the 6th Convalescent Center was to accept soldiers from the acute care hospitals, so they could recuperate before going back to combat. The physician decides when the soldier is ready for combat. Remember, not many of these guys want to return to the mud, to the mines, and to be shot at again. Hawkeye would strike a deal. "Hey, you want to stay at the 6th CC for a while longer? Well, I've got this hootch in need of fixing up. I heard that you're good with cabinet work...."

This certainly could not be justified either morally or ethically, but he sure lived well, and I managed to inherit that.

I carefully surveyed the room, but to my surprise I could find no trace of the moonshine still that MASH's Hawkeye had in his quarters. Oh, well.

One thing bothered me. Hawkeye must have had a major problem with the commander. High on the walls and on the ceiling he had painted expressions of distaste regarding Colonel Fike's hygiene, anatomy and personality. Somehow, Hawkeye had pulled some strings and had left Vietnam early. He must have known a politician. I'm sure that he had a problem with the Colonel over this. I thought that his decorations were in terribly poor taste, and I was determined to paint over the signs. However, days passed, and there was always something else better to do, such as going to the beach.

Of course the day came when the Colonel visited my hootch. I didn't say a thing, and I hoped that Fike didn't see the decorations. I'm sure he did, and I'm sure that he thought that they were my creations. Colonel, if you ever read this book, please accepts a belated apology.

My hootch was on a beach that went as far as the eye could see in either direction. It was on a 100-foot wide strip of sparkling white sand. There were a couple of lush tropical islands a few miles off in the ocean. Rumor had it that the Hilton Hotel people had an option on the islands and were planning to build a magnificent resort after the war. The only thing marring the beauty was barbed wire.

I got a bit of swimming in, but there were three problems.

First, the current was treacherous, and once I was almost carried out to sea. We were at the very tip of a peninsula, and the current would whip around the point and take complete control as it swept you out to deep water. Several GI's drowned. It got me once, when I was just a few feet over my head. One of the nurses, Janis, stood on the shore yelling, "You can do it, Genie!" Somehow, I made it, swimming against the current. Now, after my SCUBA certification, I know that it's a stupid thing to do, and that you should swim perpendicular to the flow of the current. I was lucky that day to beat the current head on.

The second problem was the sand. It was blazing hot in midday. You couldn't walk on the sand even wearing your combat boots, much less barefoot. The only things that could stand the heat were giant lizards. They were more than a foot long, and somehow, they never burned their toes on that hot sand.

The third problem was the Koreans next door. I'll discuss their strange sense of humor later.

Although it was beautiful, I was constantly reminded that this was a war zone. Mine was the very last hootch in a row of hootches on the beach. Before I arrived, my hootch, although it was in the same place, was the next to the last in that row. The last hootch was now just a flat concrete slab. A few months before my arrival, some sappers penetrated our compound and blew it away. During the attack, a sapper threw an explosive satchel through a window. It landed at the feet of a nurse. Luckily, it didn't go off. I bet she has PTSD. This was before the nurses' quarters were the mobile homes high on the dunes.

Our bathroom was just beyond that bare foundation. It was fairly luxurious for Vietnam. Faithful to military tradition, it had rows of toilets without doors on the stalls. You quickly lose your modesty in the service. Periodically, I would be sitting on the toilet and the cleaning lady would come by. It never bothered her a bit. She would just sweep between my feet as I sat on the pot. After a while, it didn't bother me either.

A refuse dump was about 50 yards from my hootch, but still in the perimeter. Once a year the dump would be hit with explosives. Now why would somebody risk his life to blow up trash? It was our theory that this was a graduation exercise for sappers. The story going around was that at a nearby training center for the Vietcong, their assignment, upon graduation, was to penetrate our perimeter, and blow the dump. The failing grade was death.

I felt very little in the way of personal risk. This may have been due more to naiveté than a grasp of reality. Periodically, I would hitchhike down to the air base, where they had a great library. Jeeps were available. Although I was a Major, I didn't know how to use my power to get the privileges of rank.

Hitchhiking was simple. I know that your mother told you never to offer a ride to strangers, but in the army you were encouraged to offer a ride to anyone in uniform if you were lucky enough to have transportation. This library didn't have books. It had rows of reel-to-reel tape decks. This was in the days before cassettes became popular, and what is a CD? They were around, but any hi-fi enthusiast felt they were down the line in quality. When I left Vietnam, I brought home about fifty reels of great music — mostly jazz and classical. Of course, I purchased a studio quality tape recorder from the PX. I still own this old dinosaur. You could take endless music tapes from the stacks, and make copies to your heart's content. They had jazz, classical, vocal, everything. I would sit there for hours with gigantic earphones plastered to my head. The earphone would block out all external sound, and I would hear nothing but music.

As I was leaving the library one day, an Air Force type ran up to me and screamed, "What the hell were you doing in there? You should be in the bunker."

"What do you mean?" I responded. "I was just making some recordings."

"Didn't you hear the explosion? A rocket just hit the building next to you, and blew it away."

They say that what you don't know won't hurt you. I don't believe that's true in a combat zone. I still think about that near miss today.

We all had great hi-fi equipment. We also had top of the line Nikons and Minoltas. No, they didn't have this stuff at the 6th Convalescent Center or 71st Evac, or PX either. Periodically, one of the guys would go on R & R, and we'd all gather around him and stuff his pockets with MPCs and our wish lists. In Thailand, he'd go to the real PX, the place where they had everything you can dream of, and have all our dreams shipped back to Vietnam. It was all tax free, duty free, and remarkably cheap. Rumors were that some general officers made a fortune by investing in the PX system. The GIs were pretty well protected at these places from being ripped off. Before going home on leave, I decided to buy my wife and daughter a couple of sapphire rings at the PX. The prices were great. But the clerk behind the counter was careful to explain that even though they looked good, these were synthetic star sapphires and not that great a deal. They looked good, and I bought them anyway, It was comforting to know that Uncle Sam was watching out for my best interests.

After I'd been in Cam Ranh for about a week, I got a call. "Doc, can you come down to the air base? One of the new guys is complaining of a bad headache."

A headache! What a waste of my time, but at least this patient was still alive. I got a jeep and took a run down.

The recruit had just come off the plane to Vietnam and was obviously in considerable pain.

"How long have you had this pain?" I asked.

"Oh, I've had this headache for more than six months," he replied. "It's so bad that I have to take narcotics just to make life tolerable."

"Narcotics, huh?" I thought. "Why is he bothering me for drugs? There is plenty of cheap stuff on the local market."

With a jaundiced eye I asked, "How come? Haven't you seen anybody about this?"

Then he replied, "I got shot in the head with a .22 before I entered the army. My neurosurgeon says that the bullet is right over the sella turcica. It's in a place that's surrounded by big blood vessels. They can't reach it without either killing me or causing a lot of brain damage."

"Bullshit! Narcotics for sure!" I thought. He had come to the right place. Vietnam was swimming in heroin. But then he showed me his x-rays. Sure enough, there was a bullet right over the sella turcica, the little boney cup that contains the pituitary gland. The military sometimes gets pretty desperate when there's a war on, but drafting some poor soul who already caught a bullet is extreme even for the Army. "What the hell are you doing in the army?" I asked.

"My draft board called me after I got shot. I brought in my X-rays and a letter from my neurosurgeon. The guy at the draft board told me that I was obviously unsuitable for service, but they had a quota to meet. He said they were going to classify me 1-A to meet their quota, but he told me not to worry, that before boot camp I would be examined and be disqualified. So I get to boot camp, and the doc says, 'Those dumbbells! It's too late. I can't get you out at this particular point. I have to let you go through boot camp, but before you go to Vietnam they will examine you again. They'll get you out at that time.' So I go through the whole boot camp hell. Well, I finish my training and sure enough I get examined before being sent overseas. Now, the doc says, 'It's too late; you've been in the army more than 45 days. You have to go and fight in Vietnam.'"

He was partially right, of course. Once he'd been in the army the requisite number of days, any injury he'd been found to have was considered service connected. The army now must consider him a soldier who received his wound while in the service, and take care of his medical needs for the rest of his life. Getting out of the army with a minor disability is easy. Easy, that is, if it's before the magic 45 days. After that, it's extremely hard to get out of the army, and for good reason. Of course, some of the fault must fall on his shoulders. You have to be a total idiot to allow somebody to put you through boot camp when you knew you didn't belong. I would have gone screaming to my congressman. Believe it or not, a grunt complaining to a congressman carries serious weight. When the congressman sends a letter to the commander stating that there has been a complaint, this is called a congressional. Everybody takes notice. When I was stateside, recruits would ask for congressionals for the dumbest things. It didn't matter. You had to carefully review the complaint, no matter how stupid, and make a full report to the congressman. A soldier with a bullet in his head wouldn't have spent one day in boot camp, much less fly into Vietnam.

"Those bums were too lazy to fill out the paperwork to get you out of the army," I told the soldier. "You don't belong here. I will take care of everything. The army spent $475 on your ticket to Vietnam. Now they will spend $475 on your ticket to get home. It doesn't end there, either.   Since you have been in the army for more than 45 days, they must consider your gunshot wound as a service-connected disability. It's just as if you got that bullet in Vietnam.   Now that you have a service connected disability, the army is going to take care of you, and your headache, for the rest of your life."

The 6th Convalescent Center was just that, a convalescent center. The people stationed there called it the 6th CC Zoo. I used to think that when you got injured, they sent you home to heal. Boy, was I naïve! If they thought that they had any chance of getting you back into combat, they would patch you up in a MASH unit, and then send you to Cam Ranh to complete your recovery. At that point, all sorts of strange rules went into action. If you had only a few weeks left before DEROS, then home you went. If we could patch you up, then back to the war you went. If we had to send you to Japan to do the repairs right, going home also depended on your DEROS. They didn't send you back to Vietnam unless you had a lot of time left. There were a few guys I tried to send to Japan for treatment of refractory athletes foot (Jungle Rot), and I would time it so that they could then go directly home. Many of the grunts had problems with Pilonidal Cysts.

These are oil glands in the crack between your buttocks. In the heat, humidity and dirt, the glands would get plugged up, and then swell. The surgeons would recommend surgery to resect the gland, but try to time it so that the GI would go home rather than return to battle following recovery.

It was up to the docs to determine who was capable of returning to combat, and who should be sent back home. We had God-like power. We could send anybody home. We could send anybody home except another doctor, or ourselves. If it were not for this limitation in power, Vietnam wouldn't have had any medical services. We exercised our power freely. We stretched the rules to send every grunt home we could. Of course, we were kidding ourselves. For every guy we sent home, they replaced him with another poor soul. I guess we all had our own motives for this behavior. By this time, everybody was questioning the sanity of this war, and we were doing our part to send our boys home. I don't think that there were any doctors in Vietnam who felt that every war was unnecessary. Those guys were all in Canada.

Physical wounds were not the only injuries treated at the 6th CC. If you developed PTSD, (Post Traumatic Stress Disorder) it was imperative that they get you back to the war for your own good. PTSD has been present in every war – even when the Greeks burned Troy. Only the name has changed. Depending on your war, it has been called "Shell Shock," "Combat Fatigue" or "Battle Fatigue." Homer even had Achilles suffer from PTSD in the *Iliad*. Jonathan Shay wrote a wonderful book, *Achilles in Vietnam: Combat Trauma and the Undoing of Character*. His thesis was that Achilles suffered the same psychological changes as the typical fighting man in a modern war. Shay showed how a soldier loses confidence in his leadership, and then, just as with Achilles, goes berserk when a buddy gets killed in action. In the *Iliad*, Achilles spears every enemy in sight, refusing to take prisoners. In modern wars soldiers charge machine gun emplacements with no regard for their own life. In World War I and World War II, we sent the affected soldiers home to return to civilian life. Many never recovered. They remained totally ineffective individuals, forever haunting the psych units at VA hospitals. By letting them rest for a few days and then sending them back into the fight, they would recover their self-esteem and had a chance of becoming whole again.

Imagine being dropped off in the middle of a jungle. You and your buddies are thousands of miles from civilization, and maybe hundreds of miles from other friendly forces. You find a tempting path in the jungle. You won't have to use your machete that much to cut your way through. If your lieutenant is smart, he will avoid that path and go the hard way. Because buried in that clear path are mines such as Bouncing Betties, or trip wires to grenades, or pungi sticks. You rotate the position of "point man" – the first man in. The point man knows that every step he takes may be his last one. It's easy to go insane under this pressure. One saving grace is that you know that you have 365 days "in country," and then you're home safe.

One year of terror is a very long time. It's one year without real sleep. To sleep soundly is to die. In combat there are only the "quick and the dead." The year passes, and you go home. But your brain stays in the jungle. This hyper alert state never resolves. Your spouse sleeps in another bed. Either that or she chances being assaulted when you have your nightly bad dream. It is now more than forty years since the war, yet I still have patients who, when they disrobe, reveal that they're packing a .45 cal pistol in their belt, or in a shoulder holster. I don't criticize. The pistol comforts them. It gives them a sense of security, and allows them to function in society. They're not dangerous; they just need the comfort of knowing they are armed.

The 6th CC was opened in November 1965. In its first year of operation it saw 7500 patients. Our census averaged more than 1000 per month, with malaria as the cause of more than 50% of the admissions. What surprised me was that 96% of these soldiers were returned to active duty rather than being sent home with their Purple Heart.

According to the historical records I've reviewed, the 6th Convalescent Hospital began with 1,300 beds, and 67 nursing personnel. By the time I got there, it was certainly reduced in capacity. I guess the war was closing down. Vietnam had field hospitals and evacuation hospitals, but this was the only convalescent center.

At any one time, we had a patient population of about two hundred, give or take fifty. We had six doctors at the hospital, but since the colonel didn't see patients, it was left to the five of us to split up the patients. A coarse approximation was that there were about 15 hard working nurses. Each morning, I'd get up to make my rounds, seeing thirty to fifty patients. Normally, this would be a horrendous patient load, but this was not an acute care hospital. All these guys were just recovering from their wounds, and just needed to be seen each day to make sure they were getting better and didn't have any wound infections. Rounds would take me about two hours, and then I would have the rest of the day to myself. I could hang around the music library at the Air Base, go swimming in my backyard, or if I got ambitious do some exercise. The nurses did all the work. They were on the wards for twelve hours. They changed dressings, gave medication, helped patients with their letters home, and only called me when there was a problem.

The combatant lived in terror that every day would be his last. The average combatant remained free of drugs since he had to keep his wits about him. Many of the non-combat grunts had turned to heroin to while away hours of boredom. It was the support troops who were stoned out of their minds. I was told that a combatant on drugs was considered a high risk to his buddies. If a combatant was stoned, his buddies would see to it that he walked point every day. The guy who walked point, was the first in line walking the jungle. Naturally, he would be the most likely guy to make contact with a mine or a bullet. Ultimately, he would be killed in action, so that the remainder of the group would be that much safer. What about the other four guys who served as support for each combatant? Theirs was a life of boredom. In my case, long distance running helped, but even that got boring.

The men stoned on drugs were not the only ones killed by "friendly fire." Occasionally you would get a gung-ho lieutenant or captain who loved to look for firefights. Not only would he look for trouble, but rather than laboriously cut through the jungle, he would unwisely lead his men down paths that were likely booby-trapped. These officers not only unnecessarily risked their own lives, they risked the lives of the men they led. The rumor was that these officers would get fragged: blown up by a "friendly grenade."

It was evident that the average soldier was not planning to help win a war. By now he had learned of the lack of support and respect from home. He was just doing a minimal job, hoping to get home in one piece at the end of his tour. There was lack of respect for authority, and certainly lack of respect for anybody who put the grunt in harm's way unnecessarily. The gung-ho officer who put him at risk was as big an enemy as the PAVN.

We Are Little Children

One night, we broke into the storeroom and liberated several gallons of white paint. Our base had a giant water tank. It was not one of those little things that you see sitting on a tower in a small town. This 100-foot diameter tank sat on the ground on a small hill about 100 feet from my hootch, and appeared to be a contribution from a petroleum storage facility. It was at least 50 feet high.

We waited for a dark night. My fellow conspirators and I carried the paint up the steel ladder to the top of the tank. Each of us held on to the steel ladder with one hand, and held a 5-gallon paint can with the other. The strong wind that night would catch the heavy can of paint, and swing me away from the ladder. I couldn't help but wonder, "If I fall to my death, will Diane get a letter that her husband was killed in action?" Most likely she'd get a letter that her stupid ass husband was killed pulling some childish stupid, ass practical joke. I tried not to look down, but every now and then I'd catch a glimpse of the ground as I attempted to regain my balance. Everything seemed very far away. Thank God the tank was not perched on top of one of those 100-foot towers. Things were bad enough as it was.

We painted a giant peace symbol covering the tank's entire 100-foot diameter. The white symbol was made up of bars and a circle two feet thick. Next, we climbed up a portable wooden ladder and we painted another peace symbol on the side of the tank. The tank sat on a hill and it was difficult to manage the ladder on the uneven ground, so we had to settle for a smaller symbol on the side of the tank.

Water tank. The other symbol covers the entire top.

The colonel was furious. He insisted we paint over the peace symbol. Of course, all he could see was the small symbol on the side of the tank. He never realized that a big symbol was covering the entire top, as it couldn't be seen from the ground. For the rest of my tour at the 6th CC, I would see helicopters deviate from their flight path to take a run over our decorated water tank.

We painted the symbol more out of boredom and to show our disrespect for authority rather than a real disgust of the war. I still felt that the war was important to stop the world wide spread of communism. Many of my comrades felt otherwise. When many of us came in, we felt that we were doing a service for humanity, and the loss of life was justified. Slowly, most of us began to question these values. I was probably one of the last to feel that this was a terrible error. We were losing not only about 60,000 American soldiers, but were killing over a million Vietnamese with nothing of value accomplished. It is a miracle today that we are on relatively friendly terms with a country we so mistreated.

You *Can* Take It with You...

It was not until years later that I had to visit the Veterans Administration Hospital. I had a relatively minor service-connected disability. It was loss of hearing from exposure to the noise of gunfire. I got to meet some of the soldiers with permanent and serious injuries. People who were struggling to live with artificial arms and legs. Some of the veterans that I see in my private practice are still suffering with chronic pain from their battle injuries. The pain does not end with the dead.

"War is hell," but at times it is necessary when all diplomacy fails. Nobody argues that the Second World War was not necessary. Together with England, we saved the whole world, including ourselves, from a life of brutal slavery under Hitler. In Iraq, we stopped a tyrant from killing his own people, and then gave the people a choice. They could vote, and form their own government, whether it was a theocracy or a democracy, it was their choice. What choice did we give the Vietnamese? If the North won, they had communism. If our side won, they had a dictatorship. No wonder we had lack of support.

We left Vietnam more than thirty years ago, and yet I suspect that that peace sign is still on top of that tank. It is probably the largest peace sign in the world and belongs in the Guinness Book of World Records.

The Army runs by rules, has no humor, and little tolerance for shenanigans such as painting peace signs on water tanks. We stole Army property, defaced Army property, and wasted Army time. Many would ask, "Weren't you afraid of the consequences?"

The refrain in these circumstances is always the same. "What are they going to do to me? Send me to Vietnam?" Here we were, in the lowest circle of Dante's Inferno. We were secure in the knowledge that there was no other way but up. Many soldiers volunteer for combat, knowing that, at least here, the Army's rules are relaxed. You're already in hell, and they don't know how to make it worse.

Bitter Medicine

6th Convalescent Center

Mai

My Beach

Nurses after a tough day

CHAPTER 8

HAWAII R & R

I got to see my wife twice that year. Once when I went on R & R, and once when they let me go home on leave. I waited until the end of the tour before I took these breaks. The year was hard enough. I didn't want to use up my leaves and then have a long stretch ahead of me when I wouldn't see my family. Most of us had these little maps of Vietnam divided into 365 segments. Each day we would pencil in a segment, and we could see how much we filled in, and how much we had to go before we returned to the real world.

There's a lot to be said for this system. You knew that you owed Uncle Sam 365 days. He even threw in a couple of holidays. You just had to survive your tour, and you were back home.

Contrast this with WW II. You went in for the duration. You stayed until we won, or you died. If the war lasted ten years, and you survived, you were in for all ten. Imagine the effect on morale.

Not all of us got the same deal. While at the 6th Convalescent Center, I interviewed an army pilot who was healing from a gunshot wound in the foot. This is a suspicious wound since it's not uncommon for somebody to shoot himself in the foot to get out of combat. "Please, doc, you gotta get me out. I've been wounded twice, and sent back twice. I know that next time I'll be dead."

"Wait a second," I said. "You're a Loach pilot. You volunteered for that job."

A Loach, the smallest helicopter in the service, is unarmed and used for reconnaissance. Small and maneuverable enough to fly under the jungle canopy, it's used to search out the enemy. It has been said that you can locate the enemy by the site of the burning Loach.

"I volunteered to fly Loach, because they promised I would have to fly only nine missions. Every time I make my nine missions, they add another nine. Get me out!"

"Hold on," I said. "We all know that Loach pilots are crazy, and I should be able to get any of you guys out under a section eight, but you're one of the few who wants to stop flying. You're one of the rare, sane Loach pilots. There is no way I can get you out."

I swear, the above conversation really happened. I realized when this was going on, that this was right out of Joseph Heller's *Catch 22*. His was a story out of World War II, and mine was Vietnam. Only the name of the war changes, very little else.

I had entered Vietnam on September 15, 1970. It was now July, and near the end of my tour. For my R & R, I arranged to meet Diane in Hawaii. To make this date, we both had our little adventures. My plane leaving Cam Ranh had mechanical problems, and I sat around the airport at Cam Ranh for more than an hour. Finally, I received the news that the flight was canceled. They told me not to worry and they put me on a later flight to Saigon. This meant that I was late getting into Saigon. I couldn't argue. I hate flying in planes with engine problems, but now that I was in SaigonI had a problem. The plane for Hawaii was leaving in fifteen minutes, and I was still wearing my combat fatigues. The Army has some strict rules. You are not allowed to fly out of Vietnam wearing your fatigues. You can either wear a Class A uniform or civilian clothing. I didn't have either. I ran into the PX and bought a pair of slacks and a shirt. I quickly changed my clothes in the dressing room and raced to the plane. I knew that nobody was going to notice my combat boots. Dashing along, I threw my fatigues into a garbage can.

I got to the plane on time, but now a snotty little MP wouldn't let me fly into civilian territory with a mustache. I know this sounds totally nuts to any sane civilian, but the military has a very strict dress code. You have to have short hair, and a minimum of facial hair. All these rules go out the window in a combat area. I think that many guys volunteer to fight just to get away from these tight ass rules. Now that I was leaving the comfort and informality of a combat area, I had to obey the rules. I ran into a bathroom and quickly shaved off my mustache so that I could return to the line. Because I was pulled out of line, Diane got a message that I wouldn't be arriving in Hawaii, but more about that later.

Naturally, my luggage didn't arrive in Hawaii. It was still on that plane with the mechanical problems. In fact, I never got my luggage until I was back at the base after my R & R was over. I didn't care at this point. I wore Diane's Levis, and I bought a couple of T-shirts. We were in beautiful Hawaii, but we didn't see much of it. As you might guess, we spent most of the time in our room at a first-class hotel. We did the whole trip on credit cards.

We could've saved a ton of money by staying at the base in Hawaii. That would have been real romantic, with the bugle waking us up each morning. No thanks! I needed to get away from Army life.

I talked about the lack of the ordinary comforts in a combat zone, and downplayed the risks. I didn't have to exaggerate my safety to any great degree – I was not a grunt in the field.

Diane told me about the stress of managing without a husband. She was caring for my daughter, and working as a physician. She was the one who had to put up the bookshelves and managed the other repairs around the apartment. My parents were wonderful in their attitude. They were not in favor of my going to Vietnam, but they felt it was their duty to take care of my family while I was away. It was a rare event when Diane and my daughter did not eat dinner at my parent's home, just a few floors below.

I don't remember if the subject of Mai ever came up during the R&R, but after my tour, I brought back my pictures from Vietnam, including Mai, and this never became a bone of contention.

We explored Honolulu, but never visited any of the other islands. We were too busy with each other in that short week. I keep telling myself that I've got to get back to paradise some day.

The week flew by and we finally had to leave beautiful Hawaii and each other. Diane took her flight to CONUS, and I hopped the plane to Saigon. In Saigon I realized that I had a major problem. A serviceman can't fly in country unless he is wearing a uniform. I had thrown mine away.

I went to the nearest medical facility to beg a spare uniform. "One of the guys just left for the states, and left his fatigues," volunteered a grizzled sergeant. "You can dig them out of the garbage."

I pulled the fatigues out of the trash, and they really weren't a bad fit! The only downside was that it wasn't an officer's uniform. It belonged to a private. Needless to say, I saluted everything in sight. You can get into very serious trouble if you're an enlisted man and impersonate an officer. They'll send you to Leavenworth Prison for a long time. I have no idea what they do to an officer impersonating a private. They probably have never come across such an infraction.

The plane was the usual C130. No real seats, just webbing to sink into. A captain sat opposite me, so close that our knees were touching. We had no conversation, since all we could hear was the usual deafening roar of the engines. We just stared at each other the entire flight. He was looking at the oldest private he had ever seen. I could see the wheels churning in his head. "What did this guy do to be busted all the way down to private? He must have done something terrible – something just short of a dishonorable discharge."

Returning to my hootch about midnight, I undressed and collapsed onto the bed. At 0200 hours there was a knock at the door. It was the commander. "Get up, Eisman," called Colonel Fike, "we've got to get down to the air base to arrange a medevac."

I dragged myself out of bed, found a clean uniform, dressed as fast as I could, and followed the colonel into the jeep. Radar drove us to the air base at the other end of the peninsula.

The general sat at a gigantic oval table. His aide sat next to him. You guessed it: The aide was the captain I sat across from on the flight. The meeting took about half an hour and dealt with the mechanics of transporting the soldiers back to CONUS in the coming weeks.

All through the meeting the Captain's eyes bore into me. "How the hell can you go from private to major in three hours?" he thought. He tried to corner me on my way out the door. "Tell me, were you on a flight from Saigon to Cam Ranh at about 2300 hours?" He asked.

"Yes, I was," I responded, and walked passed him.

To this day he probably believes that he had run into some James Bond type. One who changes from civilian to enlisted man to field grade officer upon orders from his Majesty's Secret Service.

I thought that my little adventure getting to Hawaii was stressful until I asked Diane what her trip was like. My little adventure was a piece of cake compared with hers. Thirty years later, her pain is only slightly blunted, and when I asked her to repeat her story I could again appreciate her trauma and sacrifice. Obviously, it's just not a piece of cake when our wives travel across the world to meet us.

She said she lived for the day I would be home just as I lived for the day when I would return to my family. First, there was the R&R. You could live for that. We would have eight days, not long enough, but we would have each other for those eight days. We both counted in weeks, then in days, then in hours.

Diane worked in a clinic in South Beach in Miami. She talked to patients, checked blood pressure, did some education, and counseled and treated people with various sexually transmitted diseases. We couldn't afford her plane fare to meet me. And she groused and whined about the unfairness of it all. There were congressional junkets to Vietnam, but no special rate for wives, husbands, families, that wanted to meet their loved ones. My brother-in-law lent her the money for plane fare and she kept it in her purse.

She left her purse in the exam room and went to get some free medicine for a patient. When she came back, the purse was open and the movie tickets her brother-in-law had given her were half out. The patient was uncomfortable and she still suspected nothing until he finally left and she found no money in her purse. She called the police and tried to get them to go immediately to where he worked, but no one ever followed up on it.

Well, our good old USAA insurance kicked in (one of the great advantages of being an officer in the US Army) and she got most of the money and was able to buy her tickets.

She got to the airport hours before the flight. Our daughter was safely ensconced with my in-laws. The flight went to LA, and she had plans to call her cousin and spend a few hours with him while she waited for her flight to Hawaii. A few minutes before flight time, something happened and the flight was canceled. Diane went crying through Miami International Airport to some other desk, trying to get a flight to LA. She kept explaining to some cold, babbling head that she had to be in LA at a certain time to make the Hawaii flight, and that her husband was on the way from Vietnam and we didn't want to lose one precious millisecond. The more she cried, the colder the person became and people behind her were yelling and telling her to get out of the way. She can be tough, however, and refused to move. People were pulling her away from the desk.

A hero appeared. An airline captain in uniform grabbed her arm. He pushed her though a door and holding her hand they raced to a plane. She was scrunched in the cockpit for hours. He said something about having flown in 'Nam and wouldn't allow the wife of a buddy (even if he didn't know him) to be shunted off so brutally. But she was going to arrive too late in LA to make the plane to Hawaii.

My wife found herself racing off one plane and being hauled off to another. She told me that there was a point when hands were helping her to scramble along a wing. She said, "I just don't remember. Seats were full, and they had me sit, again, in a seat in the flight deck."

Somehow she arrived in Hawaii and by some miracle her luggage had arrived.

I was due to meet Diane the next morning. She rented a car. Diane found a deli, and bought bagels and all the accoutrements. She chose a wine and brought her treasures back to the hotel.

Her girlfriend's mother was a travel agent. The agent had booked our room. She told the hotel we were honeymooners. When Diane entered the room she found a honeymoon basket with fruit and wine. It was the same wine she had just bought. The next day, when, I arrived with a bottle that I had picked up in Guam, we found that all three bottles were identical down to the vintage year. So, of course, having the same wine, down to the year, was definitely a fantastic omen.

The next morning, Diane found her way to the base to meet me, and checked into some central area where there was a board listing the men and women who were coming in that day and who would be in the next day. My name was not listed among the arrivals. Finding a real person to talk to, she was told that her husband was not on any lists to come to Hawaii for the next few weeks. She ran out of the base crying, and ran into a soldier. He said "Go back, and don't just say, 'I'm Diane Eisman.' Tell them you are the wife of Major Eugene Eisman. They probably think he's just a grunt!"

She thought "Just a grunt...what should it matter? Just a grunt...how does that differ from a major? Just a grunt...does that mean less of a man?"

And so she went back the next day. But this time, she got out of her hippie bell bottoms, her tie-dyed T-shirt and bundled up her ass-length hair. She sucked in her tears and said loudly and clearly, "Excuse me, Sir. I am Major Eugene Eisman's wife."

"Yes, ma'am!" You bet your bippy. The same slimy guy behind the desk snapped to ...and the rest is history...except for the army guy the next day who requested that she go home and dress more appropriately as we were waiting for the military transport to arrive.

One part of her experience still bothers me today. I agree that rank should have its privileges, especially since I had the advantage of being an officer while I was in the service. I had better living accommodations, fewer lines to stand in, and slightly more control of my daily activity. However, I never treated an enlisted man with disrespect, and was always considerate of everyone's feelings regardless of rank. If Diane had not returned to tell them she was an officer's wife, they would have continued to give her short shrift, and she may very well have returned home without meeting me in Hawaii. Their whole attitude changed when they discovered she was a major's wife. Why the Army finds it necessary to treat a private or a corporal as a piece of shit is beyond me.

***

Many of the guys didn't have wives to return to. They opted for a different sort of R & R. Bangkok was one of the more exciting places, especially for single guys. The place was wide open and commercial sex flowed freely. The chief of the lab elected to go to Bangkok for a good time.

Upon his return, he appeared to be a changed man. He had this 1000-yard stare. This, in spite of never seeing combat and Bangkok is not a combat zone, either. We asked him what happened, but he wasn't too anxious to relate his story. He behaved as if he was one of those veterans who'd seen too much and experienced too much, the sort of person who couldn't come to grips with his experiences and couldn't talk about it. Finally, with much prodding from his buddies, he told his story.

It appears that he had met the girl of his dreams. After painting the town red, they hit the sack. He spent this wonderful night, full of great sex, with this gorgeous young woman. In the morning they were totally satiated. She told him that she had to leave for work, but would see him again that evening. He was a gentleman, and volunteered to drive her to her job. They stopped in front of a theater where she worked. On the marquee was her picture, and her name was in lights. The marquee read, "See one of the most beautiful transsexuals in the world...."

CHAPTER 9

MEET NURSE NARK

Cam Ranh is actually a city. The army took the prime real estate — Cam Ranh Bay — as the base. The base was actually located on the Cam Ranh peninsula, whose eastern edge was many miles of broad white sandy beach. They left the city to the natives, but now this beautiful beach was off limits to the native Vietnamese.

Only as guests could the Vietnamese use our beach. Some of the enlisted men had steady girlfriends in town, and many of them married Vietnamese women from Cam Ranh. Some of the men who went through these marriage ceremonies also had wives in the states. I don't think the army knew about these marriages. A couple of times I was invited to eat at their homes, spend the night, and go back in time for rounds the next morning.

The city's population was more than 100,000. It doesn't sound like much of a city, but this population was crammed into just a few city blocks. The side streets were only wide enough to allow a donkey to pass, one way. The main street was wider, but you couldn't drive a car on it. If it had room for cars, where would you put the central sewer? How do you make a left turn across an open sewer down the center of the street?

The homes that I saw didn't have indoor toilets, and I suspect that none of the others had indoor plumbing either. On the corner of each block was a little concrete block room with a hole in the floor, and a place to put your feet as you squatted down. The toilet drained to the middle of the street, which held a shallow ditch. This open sewer ran through all the streets of the city, and to get across the street you had to walk a narrow board across this ditch. Of course, the flies and the odor were unforgettable. We've all been to the movies, and seen these city scenes, but what the theatre lacks is an odor generator. If theaters ever have such a thing, they'll also have to put barf bags in the seat pocket in front of you. You must smell it to fully experience a city without modern sanitation. (Plate X)

Public transportation got you around town. No, there were no double decker buses, or taxicabs. Public transportation consisted of a motor scooter. Attached to the scooter was a ten-foot bench on wheels. You paid 10 dong to sit on the bench and be taken to your destination. There were no seat belts. You just hung on for dear life. (Plate X)

Small stalls lined the streets. A little bigger than the typical hot dog stand, they sold all sorts of interesting Vietnamese foods. The food was cooked right in front of you. I was never interested, since I wasn't interested in catching hepatitis. At the same stalls you could pick up bargains, such as little vials of 100% pure heroin at only $8 each. They also had American cigarettes, but these were special. They were adulterated with heroin to give you that extra satisfying smoke. You would think that Philip Morris would buy up the patent. There were also stalls with shelf after shelf of army equipment, including foxhole spades, cans of insect spray, K rations – all in Army green. They were all obviously stolen, right out in the open, but nobody ever seemed to care. (Plate X)

I did get to eat out on an occasion. The French influence could be appreciated in some of the Vietnamese food. There was one little restaurant where we enjoyed a filet mignon with vegetables and wine for only $8. The filet was large, tender, and delicious. You certainly couldn't beat the price. One of my buddies suggested that the reason it was such a deal was that we were eating Water Buffalo.

Few homes had glass in the windows, so there was no barrier to flies or mosquitos. You slept under mosquito netting, or you were certain to get malaria. A barbed wire fence surrounded each home, and the windows were covered with a network of razor wire or barbed wire. And you think you have a crime problem.

I continued to do my running at the 6th Convalescent Center. One trip around was only about half a mile. It was good exercise, but boring. One of the other docs decided to run for exercise, but he was a bit more adventurous. We had a beautiful beach, so what could be nicer than a run along pristine white sand, and ocean as far as you could see?

Next to our compound was that of our allies, the Koreans. They have a great sense of humor, and when they saw this doc running up the beach, they playfully opened up with their automatic weapons. They merely kicked up the sand around his feet, but it was discouraging enough to get him to turn around and run for home.

You may be surprised to learn that I suffered a war injury. I'm being facetious of course. I was playing basketball on the beach, and I made a sudden turn to go for the basket when I felt a snap. The pain in my back was terrible, and I suffered with back pain for many years after that. The only other injury was loss of hearing from gunfire which did not rear its ugly head until I returned from Vietnam – all minor problems when compared with what the other guys suffered. It's not the kind of thing that gets awarded a Purple Heart.

Just as in Pleiku, I became close to the people around me. After all, you're living in an area about the size of a city block, and it's surrounded by barbed wire. You can leave, but:

a. There is very little to do outside the perimeter, and
b. You might get killed outside the perimeter.

As a result, your social contacts are rather limited. Everybody becomes your friend. If you developed an enemy, too bad, you were stuck with him for the duration. In spite of the close friendships I made, only one friendship survived Vietnam.

We had pretty nurses here just like in the TV show, *China Beach*. I still correspond with one of them to this day. I was at the Air Force Officers Club, with a group of doctors and nurses, and my steak was the first entrée to come to the table. I was about to dig in, when another knife and fork beat me to it. This was my introduction to the tall statuesque blond sitting next to me: Janis, the most extroverted woman I have ever met. She does not know the meaning of the word shy, and my meal was fair game.

I wouldn't say we became good friends immediately after our first meeting. We began as acquaintances. She was involved with a personnel officer, and I was just another doc. I would use any excuse to stop by and talk to her while she was sunning herself outside of her trailer. She wore this purple bikini, and I couldn't keep my eyes off her. After awhile, our duties pulled us together, and we developed a friendship that has endured to this day.

She was a free spirit, a true Hedonist. She didn't allow anything to cramp her style. She was one of the few people who didn't collect stuff from the PX. She believed in being free, and that meant being free to move with no encumbrances. Back at CONUS she lived in a mobile home in Colorado's mountains. She was a nurse in the summer, but in winter she grabbed her skis and was a ski instructor at Aspen Highlands. Skiing was her life. She worked as a nurse just long enough to support herself through a winter of skiing. Everybody knew Janis. They even named a ski trail after her. *Nark's Nook* is a short run, but if you're sane, you won't venture on it unless you're a super expert. This little run was the final exam for those that had the ambition to be ski instructors.

To describe Janis Nark as an extrovert is a gross understatement. I've been in a restaurant with her where in five minutes she's not only carrying on a conversation with everybody there, but she has tasted most of their food.

I had skied only once in my life, sliding sideways down a small hill of ice at Mast Hope, Pennsylvania. The trail was about ten feet wide and had a cliff at one edge. Every few feet there was a hydrant for snowmaking equipment. I was afraid for my life every second, and I didn't consider it fun. I told Janis my story, and she informed me that she had skied in almost every country, and the best place to ski was the Rocky Mountains. Janis promised to teach me to ski. "Just give me a call when you get to Colorado, and I'll show you what real skiing is all about."

Sure enough, a few years later one of the hospitals offered the docs a great ski trip at a ridiculously low price. Diane and I made our reservations, and then I thought of Janis, and I gave her a call.

She moved in with us for the week we were in Winter Park, Colorado. Each day she would take me to a higher and steeper hill.

I thought of her as rather a klutz. She seemed to be too tall to have good control of her body, and tended to stumble around. On skis things were different. She was spectacular on skis, and would actually dance her way over the moguls and down the mountain. I would be painfully working my way down a hill, and she would turn around, skiing backward to watch me. Then she would lift one ski, and ski backwards on her one ski while I struggled not to fall on my face. We would come back after the lifts closed, and I could barely drag my bruised ass up the stairs. On one occasion she told Diane, "Boy, we almost lost Genie today." My wife found this very comforting.

Ever since my first ski lessons with Janis, I've been back to Colorado every year. I E-mail her before I go, and sometimes we get to meet again on the slopes. She is no longer a ski instructor. She married a urologist who took her to live with him in North Carolina. Oh yes, there is skiing in North Carolina. She told me that the first time she went skiing there, she got to the top of the hill, and cried. She is now divorced.

Unlike me, she kept her commission in the Army, and ended up retiring as a light colonel. There is a downside to keeping your commission. When Desert Storm came she was activated. Her husband wasn't very happy.

***

At the 6th CC, the female nurses lived in high style. They each had a mobile home, just like the commander. They put my little hootch to shame. The nurses' homes were all in a row, high on a giant sand dune overlooking the South China Sea.

We had some time off. Janis's boyfriend and I got a bunch of steaks and lobsters from the PX. We even got a bottle of wine. I can still see us sitting at a picnic table, with a white bed sheet as a tablecloth. We gazed over the South China Sea as we poured wine for each other, and feasted on seafood and steak. I felt like I was in a Bacardi commercial rather than a war zone.

About ten years after Vietnam, she stayed over at our home. "Janis," I said, "I really have to give you credit. What impresses me most is how the nurses volunteered to go to Vietnam, and suffer all the hardships without complaints. I, on the other hand, went out of my way trying to stay out of Vietnam."

"What are you talking about?" She responded. "I didn't volunteer for Vietnam. I was bushwhacked. I was a nurse, just out of training. I went to the recruitment office because I wanted to try army nursing in a place like Germany. I told the recruiting officer that I would sign up only if I could be assured that I wouldn't go to Vietnam. The officer said, 'You couldn't go to Vietnam if you wanted to. There are too many nurses in Vietnam. You would have to get special permission from a congressman to go to Vietnam. Sign here!' Well, you can guess what my first duty station was."

After the war, she saw the same recruiting officer at a meeting. Janis charged in for the attack. She saw three other women beat her to it. She turned away, not wanting to be part of the pile-on. Obviously, this recruiting officer had trapped many naïve little girls with that story. We know that the recruiting officers have quotas. Their job is critical. They have to sell a career that promises risk to life and limb, deep/heavy boredom, and a rigid boss who's unforgiving. Still, it must be difficult for recruiting officers to sleep at night.

It's funny, after being hijacked into the service; she still kept her commission, and attained the rank of light colonel before retiring. She is a great example of the dedication shown by nurses under the stress of war. This didn't go unrecognized, and after the war was over, she was honored with an invitation to give a speech at the Vietnam memorial in Washington. That was the day when Clinton made news by having the brass balls to show up at the wall on Memorial Day. A friend of mine, who watched the coverage on television said that his only disappointment was that Janis shook hands with a draft-dodging President.

Even after retirement, she has remained active in military affairs. In 2001, she was elected to the Vietnam Veterans Memorial Fund Board of Directors. She is the only woman on the board.

Her first experience in Vietnam was almost identical to mine. She was given her assignment to the 6th CC, and when she asked how to get to Cam Ranh, she was told, "You're a big girl, find your own way."

She was not a big girl. She was a young kid just out of nursing school. But, being an attractive woman had its advantages: Hitching a ride was easy, and she got to her station alive.

CHAPTER 10

THE HOOKERS OF BOUN ME THUOT

"Eisman, how about covering for a doc who needs to go on R & R?" asked Colonel Fike. A polite request in the Army is in reality an order. A response such as: "Nah, I'm really comfortable here. We have electricity, hot showers, and I have my hi-fi set. Why would I want to run away from all these comforts and go into the boonies where people might shoot at me?" would not be appropriate. I knew that a trip to a dispensary that had only one doctor would mean that I would be giving up many of my creature comforts, but there was only one answer that was possible.

"Certainly sir, I will be happy to run off to some God-forsaken place, if this is your wish, sir."

"R & R" was our vacation. For every year in Vietnam, we all got about 10 days off to get out of the war. Some of us went to Thailand, some to Hawaii, and some to Taiwan. At Boun Me Thout they only had one doctor, and they couldn't send him off on R & R without a replacement. I was shipped to Boun Me Thuot for ten days so that the doc could have his vacation. Not only couldn't I turn down a direct order, no matter how polite, but this was a job that you couldn't refuse and still be considered a member of the human race.

In both Pleiku and Cam Ranh, I'd been stationed in the middle of a large military complex. I enjoyed the conveniences and comforts of the "city," and in addition, enjoyed the security of being surrounded by a big friendly army. Now I was going to the "boonies." There would be a skeleton of military, and little to protect us if the North Vietnamese took a liking to the real estate.

I was filling in for Dr. Hildebrand, who had two jobs. First, he gave medical support to a group of helicopter pilots. It was his second job that was most interesting: He was the doctor for four houses of prostitution. The system was simple. A girl could not work in the bar unless she carried her picture ID. Dr. Hildebrand had a book in the dispensary with each woman's picture. If a soldier got VD, he would point out her picture in the book, her card would be seized, and she couldn't work until she was treated. Every new girl had a pelvic exam before she could go to work, and the exam would be repeated weekly. If she had any cervical or vaginal discharge, she got a shot of penicillin. No fancy bacteriological or serological studies were used to make certain of the diagnosis. Remember, this was war.

It was an assembly line arrangement. I sat on a stool in front of the stirrups. The girls would all be standing in line. When one girl jumped off the table, the next would jump on, throwing her feet into the stirrups. I had one speculum, which I would soak in a pan of disinfectant for thirty seconds between exams. The situation was exactly as bizarre as you're picturing it.

This was legalized prostitution. And I have to admit the system worked perfectly. I saw only one case of venereal disease in my 10 days at the dispensary. Of course, this was before the era of HIV. It seems that, as far as we knew, Herpes was not a problem then.

To be fair, I have to compare this with my experience in Cam Rahn. Here the women were off limits, and guys were not allowed to visit the girls in the city. There was no picture ID, and no book in the dispensary. Why should there be? Prostitution was against the law. Every day we had lines of guys with drips waiting for their shot of penicillin. This was in spite of stern warnings.

My days filling in for Dr. Hildebrand were simple. I hung around with the pilots shooting pool and drinking beer. I only had to go to the dispensary when there was a problem. There were no in-patients to see on rounds, and the helicopter pilots never even had a cold. When they had combat injuries, they'd be sent to a MASH unit. The most interesting part of the job was dealing with the whorehouses. I hate to sound like a lecher, but most guys would kill for this job. The women were all young and beautiful. Their economy was in tatters, and the only way they could feed their families was to sell their bodies. In every war torn country, as far back in history as you care to go, women have done this to survive. In a war, properties and lives are destroyed, and survival takes precedence.

GIs were warned that gonorrhea in Vietnam was resistant to penicillin. This was only a half-truth. Gonorrhea responded to penicillin, it just took a hefty dose. Soldiers were told that we couldn't send an infected GI home to spread disease in CONUS. Therefore, anybody with gonorrhea would be sent to a place called *Pecker Island*, and his family would be informed that he was killed or missing in action.

"No!" you'd say. "Nobody would fall for that story." But remember that most of these guys were only 18 and 19 years old. They were from little towns in Ohio or Kansas. They really believed this bullshit.

What did all this accomplish? Well, nobody with a urethral discharge would present himself for treatment until they were in absolute agony. Being sent to *Pecker Island* was more feared than a firefight.

Black Syphilis

About this time, I sent Diane a tape explaining that we were having a tough time with *Black Syphilis* in Vietnam. Like many of my buddies in Vietnam, instead of writing letters, I would send audiocassettes home. It was easier than writing, and my handwriting was illegible anyway. Besides, hearing a familiar voice was great for morale. It took about ten days for a tape to get to CONUS, and another ten days for the reply to arrive in Vietnam.

While I was in Vietnam, Diane was working for the Dade County Health Department in Miami, Florida. At the time she was working for the division of Disease Control.

105

"What the hell was *Black Syphilis*," she thought.

She asked the Head of Disease Control, and he was concerned. What were our soldiers bringing back to the states?

"We had better ask central in Atlanta, Georgia," he informed her. This was the famed Center for Disease Control (CDC) for the entire United States. It is an agency of the Department of Health and Human Services.

When they claimed ignorance, Diane bounced it up to Paris. This was the World CDC, the health department for the whole world. Still nobody had ever heard of *Black Syphilis*.

Meanwhile, she had sent a tape to me, by return mail, requesting further details. Twenty days later she got her reply.

"Oh, '*Black Syphilis*?' Why, I just made the disease up," I responded.

At this point she felt that silence on her part would be the better part of valor. Slowly, questions about *Black Syphilis* died out.

I was reading the letters section of the *New England Journal of Medicine* around 1995, and I came across a letter that asked, "What ever happened to the *Black Syphilis* that was picked up in Vietnam?"

Dr. Hildibrand's Clinic

Dr. Hildebrand's clinic was amazing. It was an invisible hospital. You entered the hospital by crouching down and almost duck-walking down a long tunnel. There was nothing to be seen above ground except for a few pipes that acted as air vents. After about fifty feet of tunnel, there was a small emergency room. Branching off from this central room were an X-ray room, a radio room, and dental office. Finally there was a long tunnel holding about ten beds for continuous care. This entire hospital was deep underground. Before I saw this, I thought that only the North Vietnamese could do this sort of thing.

Even though this was out in the boonies it had some conveniences that we didn't have at the 6th Convalescent Center. Here and there around the camp were piss tubes, pipes sticking up about 45 degrees from the ground. Have a full bladder? No problem, just whip it out and pee down the nearest tube. There were no female nurses up here to discriminate against. We need stuff like that in CONUS.

The doc I was relieving was a captain. I was a major. That meant that every license plate on the base had to be changed. While the captain was the commander, the plates read "03." When I came to fill in, they had to be changed to "04." I really felt honored to see that an entire community had to change their license plates because I was present. Ah, the joys of command!

Still, my living conditions were primitive. I shared a room with three other men, and my bed was an army cot. I kept a fan directed on me all night long to keep the mosquitos from making a landing. You learn something every day. My helicopter friends informed me that mosquitos are aerodynamically unstable in wind velocities over a few miles per hour.

You would think that Dr. Hildebrand would've enjoyed all the girls available to him. The houses offered him as much free sex as he would ever want, but his staff said that since he was acting as their policeman, he was always careful to turn down the offers.

The city of Boun Me Thuot had a full-blown hospital about five miles from the underground clinic. Staffed by army physicians, the city hospital had about 100 beds. The docs were general medical officers who didn't have specialty training, and I was welcomed as a consultant. Every day or two, I'd take a run down there and make rounds. As I would climb into the jeep, the driver would hand me his M--16. "Here doc, you have to ride shotgun." Thank god I was never called upon to use his shotgun.

Visiting local Vietnamese hospitals, I saw stuff that I never saw before, and I never saw again. Walking a hallway in one of the hospitals, I found a young Vietnamese woman lying on the floor. She was having convulsions. Her body was arched and ridged so that only her head and heels touched the floor. The medical term for this is opisthotonos. A Vietnamese doctor was attending to her. I asked, "What's the problem?"

"I think she has Lock Jaw," he responded. This is another term for Tetanus.

This didn't quite satisfy me, so I tried to get a history. It wasn't easy. She spoke only a bit of English, and every time she tried to speak she would have another spasm, and speech was impossible during an attack. I finally got the story: Bleeding heavily with her periods, She went to a Chinese doctor. He gave her bitter tea to drink. The tea was so bitter, that she could only drink half the cup.

This started the alarm bells in my head. It is said that the most important aspect of medicine is not the physical, nor the fancy tests. It's the history. When she said "bitter tea" and Chinese doctor, "strychnine" sprang into my head.

"Aha!" I exclaimed, "Strychnine poisoning!"

I've never seen a case before (and never since) so we ran down to the hospital library and looked up the antidote. It was intravenous phenobarbital.

The next day I checked in on her, and she was doing great.

Strychnine is a natural substance, an alkaloid extracted from the plant *Strychnos nux-vomica*, and it works by blocking the inhibition of nerve impulses. These uninhibited nerve impulses become so overpowering that the victim convulses. The first effect that is noticed is stiffness in the neck and facial muscles. There is progression to a full tetanic convulsion. The body is arched so that only the crown of the head and the heels may be touching the floor. All voluntary muscles are in full contraction. Respiration ceases, and the victim dies from lack of oxygen. So if anybody ever offers you some patent medication and says, "Go ahead, take it. It's safe. It's all *natural*," you'll know better.

Making rounds at the surrounding hospitals was not part of my job, but fighting boredom was a major problem as my duties did not fill the days. I had to look for work or play.

I was the only commissioned officer at the dispensary, and quickly became good friends with the NCOs. When we'd get a break, I'd go out into the forest with them and we'd fire a few weapons to keep in practice. Besides the M--16, they brought along an M-79, which looked like a one and a half-inch diameter steel pipe with a trigger, and was used mostly for firing grenades. After I lobbed a few of those, they had me fire some flares. Finally, they handed me a shotgun shell. Imagine a 40mm shotgun shell. That's more than 1-½ inches. I aimed at a cardboard carton about 6 feet away. The spread of the pellets was so great that I doubt that more than two pellets hit the carton. The noise was deafening. I could hear very little the rest of the day, and the next morning my ears were still ringing. After Vietnam, I discovered that my hearing was deficient in my right ear, and I used an electronic stethoscope to compensate. Many years later, I lost my hearing in both ears, and required surgery. I attribute it to that experience.

I guess I've always been intrigued with weapons and explosives. I had my first chemistry set when I was six years old. By the time I was twelve years old I could have worked as a consultant for any terrorist organization.

At the ripe old age of twelve, I had become an explosives expert. Now, I don't mean the kind of expert who can tape a detonator to some C4, or a stick of dynamite. Any moron can do that. I mean the sort of expert who can go down to the corner grocery, local chemical supply house, or photo shop, and with easily obtainable chemicals whip up a batch of high explosive. With chemicals that anybody could obtain, I mixed up batches of silver acetylide, lead azide, and even mercury fulminate.

***

The night after my deafening experience in Vietnam with the M-79 was the Fourth of July. We decided to celebrate, and we went to the perimeter with an M79 and a box of flares. My buddies fired off a few, and then turned to me. "Hey doc, try a few."

So I picked up the M-79, and fired a flare almost straight up. A flare consists of a piece of burning magnesium hanging from a small parachute. As it floated toward the ground, the wind caught it, and took the flare over to where we had the helicopters parked. The cheapest helicopter there probably cost well over $250,000. I could imagine them taking it out of my salary for the next forty years. Luckily, there was no fire or explosion.

Their captain finally returned from his R & R, and it was time for me to return to the 6th CC. They exclaimed how useful it was to have an internist around, and I was a lot of fun anyway, having nearly blown up the whole base. "Why don't you come back and make rounds on the weekends?"

Back at the 6th CC, I approached the colonel, and asked if I could do that.

"What!" he responded? "Are you out of your skull? Absolutely not! We can't have our docs flying all over Vietnam, getting killed. Don't talk to me about this again." Then he stormed off.

As I've mentioned, we had a Radar type at HQ. You remember Radar, in M*A*S*H*. He was the little company clerk who could get anything done. Let me tell you where company clerks come from. It seems that lawyers have a much weaker union than doctors. The lawyers were given an ultimatum when they took their commission. "You want to practice law in the army, and be anything you want to be? Fine, just give us three years. If you give us only two years, you're anything *we* want you to be, and you won't be a lawyer." Many became company clerks.

Well, Radar overheard my conversation with the colonel. "Listen, Major, any time you want to run up to Boun Me Thuot, just let me know. I'll just type you up some orders. I have the Colonel's signature stamp."

I have to admit I was a bit shaken up. Here was this Lieutenant offering to file forged orders for me. What was the penalty for this? Was it the firing squad, or only ten years in Leavenworth? Regardless of the consequences, I couldn't turn down the opportunity.

Each weekend, Radar would type up the orders, and sign Colonel Fike's name. I would get down to the air base, find a plane, and would fly into Boun Me Thuot. That day, all the license plates would be changed to "04." I would make my rounds, and socialize with the guys. They would invite me to eat at their NCO club. There was no officers' club. Why have a club for one officer? I would sleep over and the next morning they would switch the plates back to "03." Then they would get a medevac helicopter to drop me off at my hootch.

I don't know how I kept getting away with this. Every Sunday, this loud helicopter would swoop down to the beach outside my door, and drop me off in the sand. This was in sight of the entire base and nobody ever seemed to notice. The HQ was not fifty yards from my door.

The interpreter at the dispensary at Boun Me Thuot was a beautiful and extremely intelligent Vietnamese woman, who had this thing going with a tall handsome member of the Airborne. She was not only beautiful, but she had brains and a great personality. On one occasion, her home had been blown to pieces, and when I tried to show some sympathy, she just said, "Oh, that sort of thing happens all the time. Nothing to sweat about."

She was young and had never known a time of peace. Before the South fought the North, the Vietnamese were fighting the French. On one trip to Boun Me Thuot, I was asked to see her. She was now a patient in the hospital. She had attempted suicide, and was lying in bed with an intravenous line running. She would talk to nobody, and her doctors thought that maybe I could break through her shell.

She had gotten pregnant by her soldier boyfriend, and he told her that he was already married. She had brought great shame to her family, and she saw suicide as her only solution. I stood at her bedside, and said a few words to her. She turned her face away and wouldn't speak to me. I could think of nothing to say to ease her pain, and I walked away. I have flashbacks regarding Vietnam to this day. That scene at the bedside plays over and over in my head. My only excuse is that I was fresh out of training when I left for Vietnam. There is something to be said for grey hair – the experience of caring for patients over many years. You can't get this experience from books, and only years makes one an effective physician in this regard. To this day, I remember that moment as one of my great failures.

One day, I found I had no way of getting home. There was not a helicopter to be had. I guess they were flying all over Vietnam doing more important things, such as picking up wounded. They had a "Radar" at Boun Me Thuot too. "Don't worry," he said, "I'll just type out some orders, the Captain will sign them, and we'll drop you off at the local airport."

The local airport was a grass landing strip carved out of the jungle. There was a shack at one end with a single room. This was the terminal. Along the side of the runway was the waiting room, a gazebo that consisted of four bamboo poles holding up a thatched roof. There were no walls, but there was a bench to sit on.

I walked into the shack and presented my orders to the officer behind a plywood board that served as the "ticket counter," and ran into a minor complication. The officer at the reservation desk said, "I don't understand this. You're a major. How come your orders are signed by a captain?"

Thinking fast, I explained. "Well, the highest ranking officer at the station happens to be a captain. I needed travel orders, and he issued them."

He looked at me with this really disturbed expression. It didn't seem right that a major would take his orders from a captain, but all he could do was shrug his shoulders and direct me to the terminal's waiting room.

I went over and sat in the gazebo standing beside the strip and adjacent to the jungle. There was a lot of destruction going on in Vietnam. Even the zoos were hit. We had some animals that were not native to Vietnam wandering in the jungle.

I was sitting in the waiting room. Swinging under the roof and onto my lap dropped a monster chimpanzee. He was just as tall as I was. He was strong and had very big teeth. He sat on my lap. First he smiled at me, and then he calmly ripped off each button of my uniform. I sat there, smiled back, and showed no resistance. I was not looking for a fight. After the last button was off, he grinned once more, and swung back into the jungle.

I made a total of about four or five trips. Finally, I had to say goodbye. I knew that if I continued to make these trips, they would catch up with me and I would be in big trouble. As a going away present, I was given a M-II automatic carbine. I don't know where they got it. I think it was left over from Korea.

When I was finally getting ready to DEROS, I had thoughts of taking the weapon with me. I could field strip it, and hide it in my hi-fi speaker cabinets. I would be the only guy on my block back home with a machine gun.

The chief of the lab's DEROS was a couple of weeks before mine. We were told that we could take one pair of fatigues and one pair of combat boots home to CONUS. The lab chief snuck a poncho cover into his baggage. The poncho was just a sheet of canvas that's used as a raincoat. It was easily worth about $1.50.

They found it, and practically threw him in jail. After I learned about that little incident, I had second thoughts. If they make such a fuss over a sheet of canvas, what would they do with me if they found the machine gun? I left it in Vietnam.

CHAPTER 11

MAJOR EISMAN AND THE JUNKIE REVOLT

The colonel at the 6th Convalescent Center was a hematologist who reminded me of the first commander in *MASH*, Lt Colonel Henry Blake. Good natured, but a bit unsure of his position as commander. He was sort of an amateur soldier / doctor who I thought was way out of his depth. I couldn't help but think, "What was the Army thinking when it put this guy in command?"

Docs should not be trusted with weapons, especially automatic ones. A couple of weeks training stateside at Camp Bullis won't turn us into warriors. The 6th Convalescent Center was relatively secure because it was surrounded by several companies of well-trained combatants. We were not issued weapons. Weapons, however, were just as readily available in Vietnam as heroin. Many of us had weapons stashed away in our hootches. The chief of professional services at the 6th CC, an internist like me, had an M--16 stashed in his hootch. One night we had a yellow alert, which meant that someone was trying to penetrate our perimeter. The chief put a clip in his rifle, and chambered a round. Later that night, the alert was called off. He dutifully removed the clip, and put his rifle in storage under his mattress.

Now 24 hours pass, and the chief is sitting watching his TV. Playfully, he pulls his M--16 from under his mattress and aims carefully at his TV. The TV is mounted high on the wall. You and I remember that single round he had left in the chamber. He didn't. He was not such a great shot. He missed the TV and put a hole through his roof.

To be fair, I must state that docs were not the only ones who were clumsy with weapons. At intervals along our perimeter, we had towers topped with guard posts, which were 8"X 8' platforms topped by a roof.

One of the guards told me about one of his near death experiences: He was standing guard, armed with an M-79 grenade launcher. I should remind you that these weapons look like they're stamped out of thin gauge sheet steel. They look so crudely made that one could easily believe that the army got them at the five and dime store. This soldier fell asleep on duty, sitting on a chair. You can get shot for doing this, and he was. You see, he fell asleep with his chin over the barrel of his weapon. The safety lever, which is a piece of steel with the same gauge as household aluminum foil, moved from "safe" to "armed" position. The weapon fired, and the grenade knocked him off of his chair. The grenade struck the roof and then fell at his feet. It seems that the grenade must travel a certain distance before it's armed, and it was his luck that the roof was just low enough to keep the grenade safe. I bet he never fell asleep on guard duty again.

One day the colonel approached me and said, "Eisman, you will be taking over for the next few days. There has been a change in the mission of the 6th Convalescent Center. While I am gone you will be in command, and your main duty will be to discharge all the patients. I can't say more, but we will be changing the mission of the 6th CC. You'll learn all about it when I get back."

I had never been in command of anything before, and although I always thought of the colonel as incompetent, I was certainly even less competent. I considered my position as Chief of Professional Services, a title of honor. I felt little responsibility, and certainly did not run a tight ship. For now, I got by, however, since the only challenge I had was to discharge 300 patients.

Janis and I made rounds together. We acted as mutual support for each other when things got impossible. This was one of those impossible things. She would read off the name, and list the soldier's problems. I would indicate whether he'd be discharged to CONUS, transferred to an acute care hospital, or sent back to his unit. Radar followed us around with his clipboard. It was up to Radar to somehow accomplish these discharges and transfers. I just gave the orders. We did this in 24 grueling hours.

As Chief of Professional Services, my duty was to command the physicians and nurses that served under me. You might think that's a piece of cake. After all, I was a major, and except for the chief of nursing, the rest of them were lieutenants and captains. But, command requires skills that I just didn't have and hadn't been trained in. At night the nurses would have problems with a patient, and require a doctor for orders. A rotating night call was the logical step. The only problem was that the doctors would disappear at night, and the nurses couldn't find them. I was in charge, so the Chief Nurse would collar me, and say, "Do something!" So, I requisitioned a field phone and had wires strung to every physician's hootch. The idea was that each night the phone would be handed over in rotation. Naturally, the phone got lost. So did the doctors. The solution was simple. I made myself available every night, and gave up on having a night call that included the other doctors. Problem solved, but that's not the way to command.

As Chief of Professional Services, I was to attend a staff meeting every Thursday in the Colonel's boardroom. You might think that this is simple. Just put it on your calendar. The problem was that, to me, every day was like every other day. There were no Tuesdays, Wednesdays, or Thursdays. In my entire time in Vietnam, I was able to make only one meeting. I don't think I was really insubordinate. It's just that every day was like any other day, and I just could never keep track of the meetings. I'm sure that made the Commander happy with me.

Then, to my relief, the colonel returned, and removed the mantle of authority from me. Now I found out what the new mission was.

It would be an understatement to say that we had a problem with narcotics in Vietnam. You have no idea how bad the situation was. Soldiers flew home on commercial airlines, and after a couple of hours of flight, they would go into withdrawal. They called it "the Joneses." They would become violently ill, become combative and vomit all over the plane and the flight attendants. The plane would have to make an emergency landing in Japan to off load the sick. This was happening on a regular basis.

These men were returning to CONUS with major drug habits. The heroin in Vietnam was 100% pure, and nobody was bothering with needles. This stuff was so good, that all you had to do was snort it just like cocaine. As I've said, five grams of 100% pure heroin would cost only about $8, and I believe that many volunteered for Vietnam just to get the good stuff. Something had to be done. The flight attendants didn't mind flying into country and taking the chance of getting shot. What they couldn't take was these guys going through withdrawal, going crazy, and vomiting all over them.

Now back to our mission: We were to become a narcotics hospital. Every soldier who left Vietnam would have to pee in a cup. Witnesses watched them urinate so that there were no shenanigans. If heroin or its byproducts were found, they would be sent to the 6th CC. (Plate X)

Several things were explained to me: First, I was the new Chief of Professional Services. I was second in command. Second, these guys would be incarcerated in this hospital against their will, but it must not be thought of as a prison. After all, these were American soldiers. We would have guards, but they wouldn't carry weapons. A simple fence would surround the hospital. While the fence was topped with barbed wire, the bottom of the fence was set in sand. As far as security went, this was a laugh.

All of us recognized the weakness in the plan. We were taking a bunch of battle-hardened guys who were on their way home, and telling them that they couldn't go home. We were putting them in what we called a hospital, but everybody knew was a prison, and this prison had walls of paper. Furthermore, our patients were addicted to 100% pure heroin. We voiced our objections, but were told that this was not up for discussion. The plans had come from the Gods, which meant some one star general.

Vietnamese men did the construction. They acted as subcontractors and managers. The little 90-pound Vietnamese women did the actual work. The women carried the cement block and the lumber, did the carpentry work, and the roofing. The men leaned against a convenient wall and directed.

Every day, each soldier would give a urine specimen and it would be tested for narcotics. He could not leave for CONUS until his urine was free of narcotics. That meant that guys who expected to be home with their families were stuck in Vietnam well past their DEROS. When entering our facility, each soldier was given a choice. He could be placed in a special unit, and supplied with methadone, and then weaned slowly from the methadone, or he could go cold turkey off the heroin. Naturally, if he went cold turkey, he could be home in a matter of days. If he chose methadone, his urine would remain positive until he was weaned from the methadone. He might be in Vietnam for years.

Would he be cured when he arrived back home in CONUS? Of course not! The army figured that they'd address that problem at a later date. The problem was horrendous. We were sending all these junkies back to the states. To my knowledge, there was no special rehabilitation program set up to even attempt a meaningful cure. One day I was asked to speak to a U.S. congressman. (Yep, you guessed it. I don't remember his name). He asked me how serious the problem was, and I told him how many guys we were admitting each day. I expressed my opinion that the North Vietnamese were doing more harm with heroin than with bullets. After exploring the problem, he asked me what the solution was. I told him I had no answer, and that narcotics were going to be a major problem long after we left Vietnam.

Many of the guys wanted to share with their buddies at home. These little vials of heroine that the guys bought in the stalls were of just the right size to fit in the cassette boxes we were all sending home. It wasn't long before the Army figured out what was going on. I got the story straight from a mail clerk. Now, you'd think that it was some alert mail clerk who felt that an outgoing cassette didn't feel right, and discovered that a GI was sending heroin home. Wrong! This scheme was uncovered when a buddy at home shipped his empty vials back for a refill! They found other ways of getting the good stuff out, however. I heard rumors that heroin was shipped with bodies that were being sent home.

A few of the men were truly innocents. I interviewed one GI who was from a little town in Kansas. "I'm only 18, and from a little town," he said. "So when my buddies came over to me and said, 'Hey, want to try some shit? This is real good shit.' I didn't know what 'shit' is, and I wanted to be one of the gang. So now I'm a drug addict. If I knew that that stuff was heroin, I would never have gone near it."

Of the soldiers we admitted each day, about 95% chose to go cold turkey. This was not a pleasant experience. Every bone in their bodies would ache. They would have diarrhea, nausea, and vomiting. Relieving their pain with narcotics was obviously not the thing to do. All we could do is load them up with Valium to try to ease some of the symptoms. I asked one of the patients if the Valium helped, and he responded, "You know how it hurts to put your hand on a hot stove? Well, imagine if you were made real sleepy with Valium, and then put your hand on a hot stove." So the Valium was not that effective.

Things did not go well. These guys were ducking under the fence at night to get drugs. Many of them never seemed to get clean. They wanted to go home, and we wouldn't let them.

I believe that Pvt. Mortensen is still there today. We would get him clean, and then he would fail the last urine test just before he got on that freedom plane. Back to the hospital he would go to dry out again.

****

At the Sixth Convalescent Center I could feel the black soldier's anger against whites. They would band together and riot as a group. Often I was told that they were angry, not because they couldn't get their narcotics, but because they were being forced to fight in Vietnam while many of the white men found ways to avoid the draft and were home with their families. Several African Americans told me that they were fighting the white man's war, while the Clintons and other well-off whites were using every influence they could garner to stay away from the fighting.

****

My inmates (oops patients) were furious. They were past their DEROS. Their tour of duty was over. They should've been on that bird back to the real world. After all, was their addiction their fault? Of course not, they thought, it was entirely the army's fault. The army sent them to Vietnam and turned them into addicts.

As comfortable as we tried to make it, a prison is a prison. Plenty of beds, but no privacy. Every day was like every other day in a compound surrounded by a high chain-link fence. The Red Cross supplied some amenities and there were occasional visits from state-side entertainers. I even saw a couple of visits from local girls from Cam Ranh City, but this was not freedom.

Transportation to CONUS was often delayed. Soldiers did not clear the narcotics in the urine, or sometimes there were just not enough planes. The "hospital" would become crowded and tempers flared. There was only one logical response: They rioted and burned hospital buildings. Many responded to stress the way any druggy would respond. They broke into medicine cabinets and swallowed everything they could find. They swallowed aspirin, Tylenol, and any other capsule or tablet they could get their hands on. We used all the Ipecac (an emetic to induce vomiting) we had at the hospital. We even exhausted the supply at the Air Force hospital. We had to have Ipecac flown in from CONUS.

At the start of the riot we sent the Red Cross girls off to safety, and as Chief of Professional Services, I entered the compound to see if I could quiet things down. First, I checked on the special unit, and made sure the nurses were okay. Janis was there and assured me that everything was okay, but I could see the concern in her eyes. I'm sure she would've felt a lot more comfortable with a .45 colt strapped to her waist. Then I went to the other units, and was soon surrounded by screaming GIs demanding to go home.

I finally found a table that I could climb up on. That way I could get above the crushing crowd. I pulled out my radio, and called HQ. The commander was happy to hear that I was still alive, and wanted to know if I was okay. I assured him that I was fine, and had everything under control. Nothing was under control, but I didn't know what else to say when I was within earshot of the crowd. I'm sure the commander heard much of the screaming from the grunts over my Walkie-talkie, and he knew I was lying. They kept demanding to go home, and I kept telling them that it was out of my hands. I had my orders, and nobody goes home stoned on heroin.

After about twenty minutes of this stalemate, the commander finally figured out that I wasn't going to get anything under control, and that I was in deep shit. He ordered me to tell them that everybody was going home, and that he'd get transportation in the next 24 hours. He emphasized that this was a direct order. After this promise, everybody calmed down, and I was allowed to leave.

I asked the commander, "How could you let these guys go home while they're still high?"

"I was afraid I was going to lose a doctor, you idiot."

A few days later I was called to HQ for a commendation. After being lauded for keeping my cool during the riot, there was a pause. Then using my best Peter Lorre voice I said, "But I like fires."

CHAPTER 12

HOME FOR A MOMENT

About this time I had only two months left in Vietnam, and I had had enough stress. It was time for my second vacation, my "leave." This time I wouldn't be meeting Diane in Hawaii, I could go all the way home and see my wife, daughter, parents, and friends.

The average civilian probably believes that the good old US Army pays your airfare in and out of the country. Not true! You get a free ride in, and a free ride out, but only when you are assigned to your next station.

I went down to the airport and paid my $550 (a lot of money in those days) for my ticket and made my reservations. I counted the days off as my leave approached. I couldn't concentrate on my work. You don't realize how homesick you are until you have this carrot dangling in front of your face. There seemed to be more sand in my bed, the temperature seemed hotter, and the boredom more intense. I don't even have to even mention how uncontrolled my libido became.

A few days before I was scheduled to go home on leave, Radar came to see me: "Listen," he said, "I have a great deal for you. It will save you a bundle of dough. We have a soldier that has to go medevac to the states. I can fix it so that you can accompany him. That way you'll be flying military transport all the way, and it will be free."

That was great. I gave up my reservation, and my ticket, and I was $550 dollars richer.

The day before the flight, the colonel approached me, and put his hand on my shoulder in a fatherly way. That was out of character, and I knew that somehow I was in serious trouble. "I don't know how to tell you this Eisman, but it's against regulations to go on leave by flying medevac. I don't make these dumb rules, but you will have to get home some other way."

The news hit me like a ton of bricks. How could the Army have such a stupid regulation? How could I think this way, knowing that the Army has thousands of stupid regulations? Now, I had no reservations, and no tickets. It looked like I was going to spend my leave in Vietnam. I thought, "Surely my family will understand." The only thing I could do was to go down to the air base, with my luggage, and ask if there was any space available. Then I would have to pray for an empty seat in the next few days. I could imagine the days ticking by as my leave was consumed while I hung around the airport for an empty seat that never came.

To my surprise, my luck had changed. There was an empty seat on the next flight, and I would get to go home after all. Not only that, but the trip would be free. I was not only flying free to CONUS, but my entire flight across the United States was free since I was able to fly "space available" all the way back to Miami. All I had to pay was $12 for some bus fare.

The rest of the public tended to treat soldiers like baby killers, but I have to credit the commercial airlines for bending over backwards to treat us right. Not only were we allowed to fly free, but they also put us in first class all the way back home. I felt like a king flying in luxury, like the CEO of a big corporation.

I walked into our Miami apartment around midnight, and the first one to see me was my daughter. (We never were very rigid about bedtime). She stared at me with this quizzical expression for a good ten seconds. I could see that she was wondering why this strange man was standing in her apartment so late at night. For a young child, one of our years is like ten of hers. I was now a stranger. Then I saw her expression change to recognition and she yelled, "DADDY, DADDY, DADDY!"

We got her to bed a bit early, for once, and then tried to make up for lost time.

I actually had some difficulty getting acclimated to civilian life. In Vietnam, I had spent about ten months being driven around. Sometimes I was the passenger in a jeep, but most of the time I was sitting in the back of a truck crammed in with a bunch of other men. For the first time in almost a year, I actually got to drive a car again. I could explore anywhere in the city with safety, and there was real air-conditioning everywhere.

I finally got to get a real haircut from a real barber. This guy was a character. All he could talk about was the miserable job my previous barber did, and how he should lose his barber's license. His parting words to me, as I left his shop were, "It looks like he put a bowl on your head and cut around it."

It wasn't until I was on my way home that I remembered: The previous barber had been a Vietnamese civilian who hung around the base. I remember him putting a bowl on my head as he cut my hair.

I suffered the usual refrain from Diane. She continued to accuse me of volunteering for Vietnam. She felt that I had probably chosen Vietnam as a great adventure. She still couldn't believe that they took married men, and needed internists rather than just surgeons in Vietnam.

The days flew by, and it was finally time for me to leave the luxury of Miami Beach, and return to the other world. It was around May 11th when Diane said, "Look, it's only two more days to Mother's Day. Surely you don't have to leave Mom before Mother's Day?"

I thought for a moment. "Ah, they won't miss me. What's a couple of more days?" Besides, I was really not ready to leave civilization and I exclaimed, "I can't see why not. They won't miss me if I'm a couple of days late."

So I stayed a bit longer in Miami, and enjoyed my family. Then I flew into San Francisco a couple of days late. You have no idea how many guys were trying to get back to Vietnam. You would think it was Paris, or Rome. I slept in the airport three more days before I could get a flight to Vietnam. By the time I finally got back to Cam Ranh, I had overstayed my leave by four or five days.

Meanwhile, Diane got a telegraph from the Department of Defense. It read, " DIANE B. EISMAN, MD: PLEASE INFORM US[STOP]. IS MAJOR EUGENE H. EISMAN A DESERTER, OR MERELY AWOL?[STOP]"

There was actually little in the way of repercussion when I returned, although the commander persisted in calling me Private Eisman for a while.

CHAPTER 13

BACK TO HELL

They tried everything to keep narcotics out of the hospital. Everything except to make the hospital secure. We needed double fences set in a concrete base – not sand. We needed big dogs, and MPs with big .45s. With the security we had, we had absolutely no control. It was as if they had filled a minimum-security prison with hundreds of hardened criminals. The problem was that the generals were right. These were men who came to Vietnam and put themselves in harm's way. Harm had come to them, not in the form of bullets or shrapnel, but in the form of a poison that enslaved rather than killed.

How could we treat these people like criminals? They were the victims. Many were totally innocent when they had fallen into the trap of drug addiction. So I tried to run an institution that was not a real hospital, but was a prison without walls. I had to deal with addicts whose habits would run hundreds of dollars a day if they were buying their stuff in the United States. Many were passive aggressive, and didn't give a damn about authority. What could we do to them? Send them to Vietnam? They were in Vietnam, and they were addicted to hard drugs. Any sort of punishment was out of the question. They made us crazy, but they were soldiers, patients, and victims, and punishment of any sort was uncalled for.

Everybody on the base had to give urine samples. Surprise inspections were common. All the docs and male nurses would line up in a field, and while everyone watched we gave our urine samples. Even the commander wasn't excluded from this little ceremony. The women were allowed the privacy of a bathroom.

I remember one soldier who did what he was told, and within a week his urine was clear of heroin. Now it was time to send him home. OOPS! We couldn't find his medical records. In the army you cannot travel without your records. This poor guy, way past his DEROS, was clean, and now he was stuck in Vietnam for weeks.

Radar took apart the record room, and yet no record could be found. Finally, on the third try, he pulled all the file drawers out and laid them on the floor. The office was a mess. There were records strewn everywhere. He found the record. It was stuck behind a file drawer. We got this guy his freedom bird, albeit a couple of weeks late. All the credit must go to Radar. He never gave up. If that record hadn't been found, I am convinced that poor guy would still be in Vietnam today.

I was near the end of my tour, and it was time for the yearly graduation ceremony at the local sapper school. Sure enough, not only did our garbage blow up, but also a big ammunition dump blew. The patients felt they were prisoners, and acted accordingly. Janis woke the GIs and tried to get them to cover. They told her to fuck off and refused to follow orders. This was typical of their attitude. They called the nurses bitches and whores and threatened them daily. The soldiers told the nurses that if they didn't kill her now, they would track them down back in the real world and kill them and their family.

There were plenty of times when I saw a nurse leaving her shift, crying uncontrollably. I would stop her, and we would talk for a little while. I would tell the nurses that even though I was not locked in with the prisoners for twelve hours at a time, I understood the stress they were suffering. I'm not sure how much I accomplished, but I had to let them know they were appreciated. I have since learned that many of these nurses are suffering from

PTSD. The experience of the abuse, the witnessing of wholesale death and torn limbs is beyond the ability of most to retain sanity.

The docs would interview and examine every new patient. On one occasion, I was surprised to see that one of my new patients was a sergeant. "How come we got you on narcotics?" I asked. "I thought that all the higher ranking NCOs were alcoholics."

He explained that they were getting incoming rockets. He dove into a hole to take cover, and there was a private. He shared his bottle of whiskey with him, and the private gave him a cigarette. How was he to know that the cigarette was laced with heroin? When it was time to check his urine for the flight home, he was caught.

Order at this hospital/prison was chaotic. Again, the colonel approached me. "Eisman, you will be in command for a few days. I'm going to I Corp."

Again, I was in charge. Now we ran into a big problem. For some reason there was a shortage of planes. I couldn't even get the guys who were clean out of Vietnam. The hospital filled up with angry, violent soldiers. The population swelled from its normal max of about 250 to a whopping 350 soldiers. Nobody had been discharged for days. They threatened to riot and burn the place down again. We were not equipped to handle this, not with a handful of unarmed guards against this mob.

Radar, the wise one, cornered me and said, "We are in deep shit, and we need help. I took the liberty of getting the colonel on the radio at the I Corp HQ. He is waiting for you now. Talk to him. Beg him to come back. Tell him we need him."

I was embarrassed. I had failed at my job and now I was crying for help. If I were a career soldier, this would certainly have meant the end of any hope of advancement. Thank God I was really only a doctor, counting the days that I would be free of the Army. I told the colonel what the situation was, and that I didn't have the foggiest idea what to do next. I had no planes, and in a matter of hours the inmates were going to go berserk, kill all of us, and then level the entire base.

I have to hand it to him. His solution was brilliant. He had us get all the food and beer we could get from the air base. He also arranged for a band. He instructed us to have a party in the hospital, and have it go on for days, if necessary. It worked! The beer and the music flowed for twenty-four hours around the clock. Nobody talked about leaving. Everybody had a great time.

When the colonel returned, he told me about the meeting up in I Corp. They decided to make the compound a bit more secure. The guards would now be armed with pepper spray. The fence would still be the same. It would remain anchored in sand so that anybody could crawl to freedom at night. There would be no double fencing, so anybody could still pass narcotics through the fence.

It took a couple of weeks for the crate of pepper spray to arrive. I remember unpacking the crate out in the open in 120-degree weather.

It wasn't long before we got to use it. Sure enough there was another mini riot, and one of the guards was being threatened. He pulled the canister from his holster, aimed at the perp's face, and triggered the spray. The spray came out in a single little spritz, and dropped two feet in front of him. I guess it didn't take the trip or the climate very well.

On one occasion, I was having a nice, friendly conversation and saying goodbye to a couple of soldiers. I asked them where they were heading. "Why, we're being sent to Germany," they responded.

"Germany!" I said, "That's idiotic. Germany is swimming in narcotics. We just got you guys clean. You will be hooked again in no time." I waved goodbye and walked on.

A few weeks later the commander approached me. "Eisman, can you explain this telex that I just got from MACV?"

It read, "BY WHAT AUTHORITY DOES MAJOR EISMAN REDIRECT TROUPS FROM GERMANY TO CONUS? [STOP]"

I pondered this for a few seconds, and then the conversation I had with those soldiers flew into my mind. Those guys, instead of going to Germany, got on the plane to CONUS. They told the powers that be that they had verbal orders to go to CONUS, and gave my name. I wouldn't be surprised if they arrived in the United States without any written orders.

I explained the whole idiotic situation to the colonel.

"Eisman, I'm not even going to respond to this stupid telex," and he walked away.

It wasn't until years later that I discovered that I was in the wrong, and had inadvertently given that order. According to regulations, if an officer of a rank above yours expresses a wish, or an opinion, that something should be done a certain way, that wish or opinion must be taken as a direct order. This, and most of the remainder of my legal knowledge I acquired watching the TV show *JAG*. If anything, that should make an officer think twice before opening his mouth.

While at the 6th CC, I was offered a wonderful deal – I thought. If I would volunteer for a dispensary in the Parrot's Peak, I would be the commander. I have not the foggiest notion of where "Parrot's Peak" was, but I'm sure it was in some isolated God-forsaken area of the jungle. However, I would have my very own jeep, and my own helicopter! Maybe the guys would teach me to fly. I would be like the President of the United States. This was every little boy's dream. No matter how old a man gets, he still has a boy's yearn for toys. A helicopter is almost irresistible in spite of the risks involved. I was tempted to just accept the assignment, and tell my family about it later, but I didn't dare. It wasn't until many years after Vietnam, that I learned that it was not Parrot's Peak, but Parrot's Beak, an area of southeastern Cambodia.

I told Diane and my parents the happy news. My father, normally very calm and collected, became hysterical. "Remember, you have a wife and a child. Don't you dare volunteer for some station up on an isolated mountain top."

I realized that I would never have my own helicopter.

CHAPTER 14

I'M NOT DEAD

The closer I got to DEROS, the slower the days passed. I was aching to see my family again. I was packed and I hung around the airport hoping to get a flight out a couple of days early.

No matter what I did, I couldn't swing it. The big green machine had me in its control. I was doomed to be in Vietnam for 365 days, not one day less, and not one day more, and that was that.

The flight back took the usual fourteen hours. It seemed like days. The flight home was markedly different from the flight to Vietnam. There was a party atmosphere in the plane. You would think it was New Year's Eve on Broadway except that everybody was singing, *Leaving on a Jet Plane*, rather than *Auld Lang Syne*.

I still had another year to give the Army. The Army wanted to favor me for my year of service in Vietnam. I was told that I could go to just about any Army hospital I desired. If my memory serves me correctly, they offered me a major medical center in California. They had heart after all. It would have been in my best interest to accept a large center, where I could receive further training. My father was ill, however, and I asked to be close to home. I was transferred to Fort Jackson, South Carolina for a year. This was a large, one story, wooden hospital. If you needed to go to the other side of the hospital to see a patient, you had to be sure to pack a lunch — It went on for miles. It was not until I was ready to leave the service that they constructed a multistory modern hospital.

I lived off base with my family, just like a civilian, and bicycled onto the base every morning. Life was safe, and easy, although I didn't care for the regimentation. No more combat fatigues and long hair. Now I had to be neat and wear a class A uniform.

The year of separation while I was in Vietnam took its toll on my family at home, and it wasn't until I was home for good that my wife told me about the impact my absence had had on my family.

My daughter's friends in preschool told her that she would never see her father again. Diane went crazy trying to reassure her that I was coming home. I'm sure that the wound from the year of separation from her father has healed, but there are many fathers who never returned. Those families never heal from their wounds.

While I was in Vietnam, Diane received an early morning call. She heard the sound of Teletype in the background. An officious voice told her that the call was from the Department of Defense. She was told that I was killed in action. Her world had come to an end. How was she going to tell my daughter that her father was never coming home?

She went to a friend of hers, crying hysterically. He was in law enforcement, and had some knowledge of the working of the military. He told her that calls like she received were common – a product of an unpopular war. The Fonda types of the world make these calls. Nobody is informed of a soldier's death over the phone. Someone of equal or greater rank would visit the home. These calls were made by pranksters or other evil people out to destroy morale.

While I was in Vietnam, once every two weeks I could make a phone call to Diane. These calls were patched to volunteer Ham radio operators in Vietnam who would transfer the calls to Ham operators in CONUS, who would patch into a long distance line to your home. You were limited to only a few minutes. By luck, I made a call to Diane the day after she received notification that I was killed. When my call was connected, I heard a hysterically happy wife on the other line.

EPILOGUE

What lasting effect has this experience had on me? I was lucky. I do not suffer from PTSD. Why should I? I never suffered the stresses of combat. However, these are experiences that never leave you. I still look up automatically when I hear a helicopter, and not a day goes by that I don't see that guy with eyeballs lying on his cheeks.

My friends welcomed me home. Nobody called me a "baby killer." At Fort Jackson the community had too much respect for the soldiers, and in Miami, I was no longer wearing my uniform. I was extremely upset over the stories in the newspapers in regard to the treatment of returning soldiers. I appreciated their hardship and sacrifice, and that many would not be returning home.

On my return home, I still believed it was a necessary war. Most of us don't get insight until many years later. The years allow us to see the consequences of our actions. How long did it take for Robert McNamara to write his book? He was at the center, and had access to all the data and he failed to realize what the future held, and that this was a war of tremendous cost and no profit.

I still feel pride in having served my country. When we went into Afghanistan to root out Bin Laden, I felt like packing my gear and going along. I know, at 66 I was a bit long in the tooth for a soldier, but as a doctor, I wouldn't expect to carry a pack and a rifle. Believe it or not, I've learned since then, that even at age 66, they would have been happy to have another doctor.

I think the people who avoided Vietnam feel that they have skipped an important part of life. They have evaded responsibility, and will never be whole until they correct this major life decision. Recently, President Clinton volunteered to pick up a rifle and go fight for Israel. Everyone laughed. They knew he was an old draft dodger and the offer was hollow. I know otherwise. He would probably do anything to re-live the past, to patch up that major defect in his history. But, as Confucius said, "You cannot step into the same river twice."

If I volunteered for Afghanistan, my wife of course, would kill me, and then divorce me. Now she would know for sure that I had really volunteered for Vietnam. After I left Fort Jackson, South Carolina we settled in North Miami, and over the years we have built our medical practice. Diane and I share the same office. She practices family medicine, and I do my internal medicine with my subspecialty in cardiology. My life is far less exciting today, but it's nice being with my family, and not worrying about being killed every day. We jump in the car to make rounds at the hospital, and I don't hand Diane the M--16 and ask her to ride shotgun. I drive all the way to the other side of Miami, and unless I go through certain particular neighborhoods, I'm not concerned about booby traps or ambushes. As you can see, you have to be somewhat concerned, living in Miami. Now and then I hear gunfire in the distance, which brings back fond memories.

My feeling is not unique. During the Second World War there were shoe salesmen, shopkeepers, etc., piloting B-17s over Europe. The risks were great, and there were many destroyed in those raids. At the end of the war, they were shopkeepers and shoe salesmen again. No longer commanding a B-17, and being responsible for the command of their men. Even though they were now safe, there had to be some sense of loss regarding their diminished responsibility. People are happy to be home and safe, but they tell war stories for the rest of their lives.

I enjoy medicine. I love the challenge in the emergency room where a patient's survival depends upon cool thinking, and sometimes I actually enjoy jumping out of bed at 0300 hours to run to the hospital. I feel honored that I have had so much opportunity not only to prolong the life of many of my patients, but also to improve their comfort. I'm not bored at all, however, if I wrote a book about my life now I would bore you to tears. It brings me back to those characters in M*A*S*H*. Several of them tried to do a sequel TV series that took place at a VA hospital in peacetime. It was a bomb!

Thirty years later, they no longer call Vietnam vets "baby killers." Society is beginning to feel a bit guilty about the way they treated their soldiers. During and right after Vietnam, there were no welcoming home parades, and no parties for the soldiers who made it home. The injured were allowed to sit in VA hospitals — forgotten.

The average GI did not volunteer during the Vietnam War. He was drafted and told by his country to go and kill. Then, after obeying his orders, he was treated like a murderer. Perhaps he felt a bit lucky that he didn't have to serve prison time for murder after serving his country.

From my observations, the majority of the grunts were black. Given the climate of the time, their socio-economic status ensured that the lower echelon were mostly black. But to be fair, I saw several officers, some field grade, who were black. So the new army is not so bad for the African American if he wants a great career.

I served as a physician, a non-combatant who tried to patch people up and keep them alive, but even doctors got some criticism. If doctors did not serve, it would be impossible to fight the war. People accused us of supporting evil by agreeing to go to Vietnam. These comments were not directed to me personally, but they were mentioned in periodicals.

Mohammed Ali voiced this opinion when he refused service. He said that he had no quarrel with the <u>Viet Cong</u>, and that no Viet Cong ever called him nigger.

Not everybody was unappreciative. Memorials were being constructed all over the United States. The wall in Washington was built in 1982, and today it is one of the most visited sites in the capitol. As I stated previously, Nurse Nark is a major mover and shaker for the Washington memorial, and I'm proud to be her friend.

I recognize that the war was a mistake, although I'm proud that I served. To some extent, I respect those who refused to go. The ones who chose jail rather than take up a weapon in that war get my respect. It takes a lot of courage to resist authority. You are truly risking your freedom, your economic welfare, and your sacred honor. They were smart enough to know what was right, and brave enough to take the punishment for their resistance. The North and South Vietnamese are now united under one communist government in spite of all our efforts. The general public feels that communism is an evil, but is it more evil than the choice we gave them – fighting sustaining a dictatorship? I suspect that the present Vietnamese regime, feeling the pressure of the present world, is slowly converting to capitalism. Who knows, the next step may be elections? We may have won without winning the war. Patience and gentle pressure may be all that it takes. It spares many lives. I have old army buddies who have returned to Vietnam as tourists. They were welcomed with open arms. This is quite a surprise to me considering the devastation we caused.

But, I am disgusted with those who chose to run to Canada, or join the Reserve to avoid the war. They are the true cowards, and I'm sure that even thirty years later, they have little self-respect.

I was not among those who braved the enfilade fire of Normandy. I did not face the Chinese in that awful winter battle of Chosan, and I never had to walk "point" in a Vietnam jungle, but I'm proud to have been a member of the fraternity.

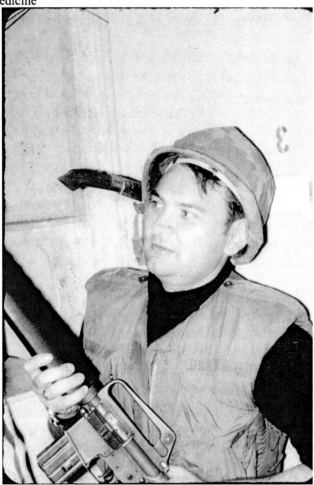

The author during a yellow alert

CPSIA information can be obtained at www.ICGtesting.com
Printed in the USA
LVOW12s0234040315

429195LV00002B/144/P